U.S. Security in
the Twenty-first Century

About the Book and Author

How will the international environment change, and what will be the shape of U.S. security policies twenty years from today? Barry Blechman answers these questions by analyzing the many variables that will influence the international arena. Some factors--such as demographic trends--change slowly and can be forecast with confidence. Others depend more directly on often capricious changes in human attitudes and decisions and thus must incorporate greater degrees of caution. Dr. Blechman assesses such factors as demographic trends, patterns of economic growth, advances in military and civilian technologies, and--most important--shifts in national attitudes and relationships among nations that will influence the making of future U.S. security policies. Utilizing Delphi techniques, in-depth interviews, and standard statistical projections of quantifiable factors, Dr. Blechman describes four plausible patterns in international relationships that would have very different impacts on U.S. security planning. He concludes that there is likely to be a continuing diffusion of international power, which will lead to reduced international cooperation, a further weakening of international institutions, more independent foreign policies, and more frequent recourse to military power. Even so, Dr. Blechman paints a relatively optimistic picture for the U.S., arguing that its overwhelming economic and technological prowess should enable it to maintain a relatively advantageous position throughout most of the world, well into the next century.

Barry M. Blechman is the founder and president of Defense Forecasts, Inc. He served as assistant director of the U.S. Arms Control and Disarmament Agency from 1977 to 1979 and has been affiliated with the Brookings Institution, the Carnegie Endowment, the Center for Strategic and International Studies, and the Johns Hopkins University Foreign Policy Institute. He prepared this study as a consultant for the Institute for Defense Analyses.

An **IDA** Book

Preparation of this book was supported
by a grant from the Central Research Program
of the Institute for Defense Analyses

U.S. Security in
the Twenty-first Century

Barry M. Blechman

Westview Press / Boulder and London

Westview Special Studies in National Security and Defense Policy

Published in 1987 in the United States of America by Westview Press, Inc.;
Frederick A. Praeger, Publisher; 5500 Central Avenue, Boulder, Colorado
80301

Library of Congress Cataloging-in-Publication Data
Blechman, Barry M.
   U.S. security in the twenty-first century.
   (Westview special studies in national security and
defense policy)
   1. United States--National security. 2. Twenty-first
century--Forecasts. I. Title. II. Series.
UA23.B544 1987   355'.033073   86-18464
ISBN 0-8133-7315-8

Composition for this book was provided by the author.

Printed and bound in the United States of America

6   5   4   3   2   1

To Jenny and Allison,
who will see a lot more of
the twenty-first century than I will;
may your scenario be an optimistic one.

Contents

Tables and Figures

Tables

Figures

Foreword

That future patterns of political/military relations are difficult to forecast is well known, of
course, and is one consideration that discourages
serious attention to long-range strategic planning.
Given the considerable lead-times associated with
the development and acquisition of contemporary
weapon systems, however, deficiencies in long-range
planning can have a serious, adverse impact on the
nation's security. This study seeks to strengthen
U.S. long-range military planning by identifying
the major factors that will determine the strategic
environment over the next twenty years, projecting
their impact on relations in particular regions and
between those regions and the United States, and
combining these possible developments on a regional basis into alternative composite, strategic
environments.

The author is grateful to Seymour Deitchman,
vice president of IDA, who encouraged this book
and ultimately made it possible. He also would
like to thank his IDA colleagues, Phillip Gould,
Robin Pirie, Paul Richanbach, William Schultis,
Victor Utgoff, and Harry Williams, reviewers
James Edgar, David Jones, Thomas Moorer, and George
Quester for helpful advice and guidance, and the
nearly 100 experts listed in the report who contributed to the several parts of the analysis. The
writer alone, of course, bears full responsibility
for the content of the book.

William Y. Smith
President
Institute for Defense Analyses

1

Planning for the Year 2001

The standard window for long-range military planning--ten to twenty years--encompasses the turn of the century, a date that attracts far greater attention than most others, if only for symbolic reasons. What will the world be like as it enters the twenty-first century? What policies and objectives will the U.S. armed forces be asked to support? What challenges will be posed to U.S. security? Although the turn of the century seems very far away and events uncertain, in fact we can predict some things with confidence.

Demographic trends, for example, the size and distribution of the earth's population, can be forecast with near certainty. Birthrates in some countries may increase or, more likely, decrease and life expectancies may lengthen or shorten, but these changes will not have a significant impact for more than twenty years and, even so, are largely predictable. The distribution of the world's economic resources is also pretty well known; with only modest hesitancy we can forecast which nations will be the primary producers of energy, of critical minerals, and of food. It is not that existing patterns will not change--simply that the period of time required for new technologies to make possible the extraction of resources from new locations or to change the relative value of different types of resources is normally very long.

We also know a great deal about the structure and capabilities of the military forces that are likely to be operational in twenty years. This is certainly the case for such major items of

equipment as warships, some of which require more
than five years to build and have a life
expectancy of more than thirty years. It takes
five to seven years to design a new weapon, and
even longer to develop one fully. Broadly
speaking, the technologies that will determine the
characteristics and capabilities of armed forces
in twenty years are for the most part already
known and already are being developed for military
applications. In an age when both great powers
relentlessly pursue potential military technologies in all scientific disciplines, technical
surprises are a thing of the past.

In short, we can describe the physical
parameters of the strategic environment at the
turn of the century with a fair degree of
accuracy. Inevitably, however, we are far more
uncertain about events and relationships that
depend primarily on human attitudes and decisions,
this uncertainty is similar to the familiar
intelligence dilemma of being able to discern
capabilities but not intentions. It is far more
difficult to make long-term predictions than
short-term intelligence forecasts, moreover,
because in twenty years capabilities themselves
can be strongly influenced by intentions.

Consider the distribution of economic
resources. The "modest hesitancy" in economic
forecasts noted above pertains largely to
uncertainties about national decisions to alter
patterns of resource dependencies. It is conceivable, for example, that at some point the
Western nations might decide to pursue a crash
cooperative program to end any dependency on
Middle Eastern oil by developing both new energy
technologies and additional means of conserving
energy. Such a decision might be unlikely, and
there is no guarantee that any such program would
succeed, but the possibility cannot be ruled out.
Similar crash programs could prove expectations
about operational military technologies inac-
curate. In the normal course of events, for
example, if the United States decided to deploy a
space-based missile defense system, it probably
would not be operational until well into the next

century; a crash, "Manhattan-like" project, however, might advance that date by a decade or more.

Forecasts of the basic relationships among the nations of the world are especially difficult. Obviously, some things are almost certain not to change. One need not be bold to predict that nationalism will remain the dominant force in humanity's scheme for organizing itself politically during the next twenty years; neither the establishment of a world government nor the creation of sovereign regional organizations seems plausible. But forecasting the relationships that nation-states will choose to maintain with one another in twenty years is quite another matter.

Consider the evolution of world affairs during the past twenty years. China and the Soviet Union, then close allies, are now adversaries. China and the United States, then implacable foes, are building increasingly close relations. As feared twenty years ago, North Vietnam has gained control of all that was once known as French Indochina, but Vietnam's gain has primarily helped the Soviet Union—not, as then expected, China, which fought one war against its former Vietnamese ally and now confronts Vietnam with major military forces. Europeans, bitterly divided in the mid-1960s between East and West, with few contacts of any sort between the two camps, now maintain a range of economic, social, and cultural contacts of such magnitude as to suggest that only an anachronistic military competition divides them. Even conservative West German politicians now speak ritualistically of the desirability of deepening this cooperation and contact. At the same time, socialists in France, Italy, and Iberia, once believed to be sympathetic toward Soviet positions, have become stalwart defenders of a tough political and military posture toward the Eastern bloc.

In short, much can change in two decades, including basic international relationships and physical aspects of the strategic environment. Both these physical and political changes can have a significant impact on military requirements and on choices among competing military strategies and force structures. Unfortunately, the very long lead times required to develop and deploy modern military forces necessitate that such choices be made in the face of this uncertainty.

This study is intended to strengthen our understanding of long-range trends in the international political/military environment and thus to aid strategic decision-making. It does not attempt to predict the strategic environment, but rather to illustrate several possibilities. These possibilities include one strategic environment that represents an extrapolation of current trends--it is more or less a picture of what the world would be like if all the primary trends evident today were to continue unchanged. But this should not be confused with a forecast of what is most likely to happen. It would be most surprising if a "surprise-free" forecast proved to be accurate. If there is one lesson history teaches, it is to expect the unexpected.

The factors that can affect the strategic environment for military planning are large in number and complex in their relationships to one another and in their potential impact on political/military relations. The first class of factors--demographic trends, the distribution of resources, trends in economic performance, for example--is largely observable and quantitative in character, and it is thus relatively easy to project the range within which these factors might vary during the period of the forecast. In considering these variables, we made use of standard sources, many published by the U.S. government, that forecast such trends in a variety of scenarios.

A second class of factors that influence the strategic environment has a similarly tangible aspect in that it depends in part on physical capacities, but also is directly dependent upon national decisions. The proliferation of nuclear weapons is an excellent example of this type of factor. Which nations will have nuclear capabilities in ten to twenty years and what the size and

character of their arsenals might be can have a
decisive impact on the threats posed to U.S.
security. Nuclear attacks, after all, are the
only contingencies that we believe threaten U.S.
territory and citizens directly; we are far more
confident of our ability to deter or defend
against attacks with conventional weapons.
Questions of nuclear proliferation thus must be
considered in U.S. military planning. The risks
of proliferation depend in part on which nations
could have access to the physical facilities
necessary to create the special materials and
build the other components necessary to fabricate
nuclear weapons; it is easy enough to gauge which
nations fall in this category. In addition,
though, there is the question of intentions:
Which of those candidate proliferators actually
will choose to invest the necessary resources to
exercise the option? The development and
proliferation of militarily significant conventional technologies is a comparable question: The
development of these technologies will have a
major impact on the strategic environment. The
rate and pattern of proliferation will depend not
only on physical capabilities, but also on the
choices of national decision-makers. We depended
heavily on Delphi techniques to forecast both
nuclear proliferation and advances in conventional
military technologies. In each case, a panel of
experts was recruited and the members asked, indi-
vidually, to answer an open-ended question about
current trends and likely developments. Responses
were tabulated and used to derive a forecast of
the future. The technique is described more completely in Appendix A.

A third class of factors is more difficult to
forecast. These are the basic societal values and
attitudes that determine foreign policies and the
relationships among nations. To forecast trends
in these relationships, we relied on structured
interviews with experts--individuals with detailed
knowledge of, and great experience dealing with,
the different regions of the world. A complete
list of the approximately sixty experts interviewed for this part of the study, many of whom
have served at the highest level of the U.S.

government or in European governments, is
contained in Appendix B. On the basis of these
analyses and economic forecasts and other supple-
mentary material, it was possible to identify both
current trends in the different parts of the world
and the major uncertainties that could cause
significant departures from the directions indicated by current trendlines.

This book is organized into five chapters.
In Chapter 2, we describe trends in several of the
basic factors that will determine the potential
leverage the United States will bring to the
international environment early in the next
century. Included are both those factors that
determine U.S. capabilities (technology, public
attitudes toward the U.S. role in world affairs,
economic growth, and defense spending) and those
that serve more as constraints on the flexibility
of decision-makers (dependencies on regions abroad
for critical resources, technologies available to
other nations, and nuclear proliferation). In
Chapter 3 we review alternative ways that events
might unfold in the different regions of the
world. For the purposes of this discussion, we
have divided the world beyond the United States
into six regions: Europe, the Soviet Union, South
and East Asia, the Middle East (including North
Africa), sub-Saharan Africa and Latin America.
For each we offer a "surprise-free" forecast and
we elaborate the key uncertainties that could
affect alternative futures. These discussions
include analyses of the fundamental demographic,
economic, attitudinal, and technological trends
that will determine events in each region--as well
as an assessment of the consequences of these
basic factors for political/military relationships. In Chapter 4 we describe five alternative
strategic environments--these are composite pic-
tures of the international security environment at
the start of the next century. One environment
represents an extrapolation of present trends; it
is a composite of the surprise-free forecasts.
The remaining four alternatives are strategic
environments that differ significantly from the
"surprise-free" forecast (and from one another) in
their implications for U.S. security planning.

Taken together, the alternatives give a reasonable bound on conceivable futures, providing both a basis for testing the adequacy of alternative military force postures and military strategies, and also a means of developing hedges against unexpected, but feasible, developments.

2

U.S. Capabilities and Constraints

More than any other single factor, the future environment for U.S. military planning will be shaped by U.S. policies and by the resources this nation brings to bear in support of those policies. As the world's largest economy by far, as a great military power, and as the political and diplomatic leader of most of the world's democratic nations, the United States can and does have a decisive impact on world events. Consequently, projections of U.S. capabilities and analyses of the factors that might constrain U.S. flexibility in international affairs are essential components in any forecast of alternative future strategic environments.

Many factors shape U.S. decisions and policymaking and determine the assets the United States utilizes to promote and sustain those policies. In this chapter, we examine four of the most important of these factors: (1) the development of military technologies in this nation and abroad--trends that will help to determine both U.S. military capabilities and the military threats posed to U.S. interests; (2) the growth of the U.S. economy, which influences this nation's basic position in world affairs, affects defense spending, and determines the extent of our dependencies on foreign nations for certain economic resources important to the nation's well-being; (3) the spread of nuclear weapons to other nations; and (4) public attitudes toward foreign policy.

MILITARY TECHNOLOGY

The rate of technological change and its primary direction are important determinants of the future strategic environment. Technological advances will have a direct impact on the military capabilities of the United States and those of its allies, while advances in Soviet technologies will contribute to the form and severity of the military threat posed to this country and its interests abroad. Technology also will determine the vulnerabilities and assets of the U.S. position in world affairs. In time, technological change can influence the relative economic power of nations and thereby modify the distribution of tangible U.S. interests around the globe. This can cause us to become more independent of some nations, but also can increase our dependencies on others. Earlier in this century, for example, tin and natural rubber were essential ingredients for the nation's industrial production, a fact that required we pay close attention to developments in Southeast Asia--the primary source of those commodities. In more recent decades, however, technological developments have shifted the output of U.S. industries markedly. Minerals found primarily in southern Africa, such as cobalt and chromium, are now of far greater importance for the nation's economic performance. Trends such as these can alter the strategic environment significantly by requiring policies to assure access to the new regions of critical importance.

The start of the twenty-first century is not so distant that one should expect revolutionary technological change. The technologies that are likely to have significant impact on U.S. security interests are well known and already are being applied to the solution of U.S. (and Soviet) defense problems. This fits with recent experience; virtually all the technologies now entering U.S. and Soviet weapon inventories were under development in the late 1960s. Several respondents who took part in our Delphi survey pointed out that given the substantial efforts

apportioned to defense research by both the United
States and the Soviet Union, "technological
surprise," as the phrase has been understood
generally, is most unlikely. As one respondent
put it, "The main trends are usually evident. . ..
The capabilities which I would expect to become
operational will probably depend less on technological factors and more on momentum (or inertia),
bureaucratic imperatives, and the occasional spurs
of conflicts."

The biological sciences are the one possible
exception to this rule. Technologies now emerging
from biological research--particularly genetic
engineering--could have a significant impact on
U.S. security by the turn of the century.
Specific applications for this research have yet
to be delineated, but there does exist a general
feeling among experts that biotechnology is
advancing so rapidly and the state of knowledge in
this field is so dynamic that there could well be
some sort of surprising breakthrough within twenty
years. To be sure, such a breakthrough would be
more likely to occur in the United States than in
the Soviet Union, because the scientific infrastructure in the biological sciences is much
better developed in the United States. There is
also a possibility that a third nation (most
probably Japan) could pursue military applications
of biotechnology.

The U.S. lead in biotechnology reflects a
general advantage in the technological competition
with the USSR. There is no reason to believe that
the United States will not be able to maintain a
broad technological lead throughout the period
under consideration. The length and significance
of this advantage, however, may be modest. Among
the most positive assessments of the U.S.
technological lead by the members of our Delphi
panel was the following: "The U.S. will, in
almost all cases, have the capability [i.e., in
eighteen key technologies] before the Soviet Union
and will maintain a technological lead. Nine of
the technologies will provide significant boosts
to the productivity of national economies. [These
nine technologies] will permeate the U.S. economy

much earlier and more thoroughly than the Soviet
economy, resulting in a net strengthening." Most
other respondents were less sanguine, however;
they assessed the U.S. lead at roughly five years
in most technologies--and perhaps ten years in
some aspects of electronics--and forecast that
those leads would remain stable into the next
century.

One respondent added a strong cautionary
note. He remarked that despite superior U.S.
technology, U.S. weapons actually performed more
efficiently than their Soviet counterparts only
when electronics constituted an essential and
significant component. Furthermore, he saw no
indication that the United States was moving to
improve its technological lead in any area and
expressed some concern that we might actually be
caught by a Soviet breakthrough in the application
of directed energy weapons (i.e., lasers and
particle beam weapons) in both tactical and
strategic applications. The appearance of
effective directed energy weapons in the USSR's
operational inventory before the end of the
century should not be ruled out, he argued, and
military planners should hedge against that
prospect. The United States, he maintained,
should be prepared to make major force structure
changes on relatively short notice.

There is also the possibility of a
technological advance which could greatly reduce
the dependence of the United States and its allies
on foreign sources of energy--a potential
development with clear implications for military
planning. One respondent suggested that a
national decision to pursue new types of nuclear
power could make the United States self-sufficient
in energy within twenty-five years at no greater
cost than would be expended in the absence of such
a decision. He suggested further that similar
decisions could reduce greatly the dependence of
Japan and Western Europe on the Middle East for
energy supplies, thus reducing the importance of
that region in U.S. military planning. Other
respondents noted the possibility that
technological advances in fusion energy also might

make energy self-sufficiency possible. No one
forecasted the development of operational fusion
energy systems before the end of the century,
however.

Basic Technologies

There are six major areas in which
significant technological advances are taking
place: computers, materials techno-logy, space
technology, directed energy, biotech-nology, and
nuclear weapons technology.

Computers. There was general agreement that
the most significant technological changes taking
place today, and the most important to be expected
in the future, are in computing capabilities.
Terms such as "computational plenty," "jumps," or
"rapid gains" in computing are commonplace in the
usually conservative responses to the survey. The
following advances in computing capabilities can
be expected to become operational with U.S. forces
in the late 1980s and with Soviet forces by the
early- to mid-1990s:

- Digital supercomputers based on
  gallium arsenide circuits with the
  potential to operate at speeds ten
  times those of the current CRAY II
  computer at the same cost
- Comparable advances in symbolic
  computers
- Computer hardware and software that
  promise to reduce tenfold the time
  necessary to design complex integrated
  circuits
- Tools to develop computer software
  that can reduce by an order of
  magnitude the time necessary to write
  programs.

These new computing capabilities will
multiply military capabilities in a number of
ways, notably by enhancing the amount of data that
can be processed simultaneously and by promising
more refined procedures for extracting pertinent

information from large amounts of data. Among the potential applications of these capabilities are highly accurate guidance and tactical targeting systems for autonomous conventional ordnance, more effective signal processing for all types of sensors, more efficient command and control systems enabling higher level authorities to direct combat far from the scene of the battle, and increased electronic warfare (and counter electronic warfare) capabilities.

An intriguing consequence of these improvements in computing capabilities is likely to be the development and military application of artificial (also known as "machine") intelligence. Just as computing improvements are making possible the use of machines to design software and complicated circuits, thus accelerating the pace of advances in computing capabilities, major advances in military capabilities can be foreseen through the use of machine "experts". Computers capable of inference and deduction based on rules specified in software packages are likely to be developed in the early- to mid-1990s in the United States and by the end of the century in the Soviet Union. Such a development would permit computers to abstract pertinent information from raw data, thus providing direct support to military commanders. For example, machine "experts" could replace human copilots or tank gunners, and assist the single pilot or tank commander by interpreting intelligence--particularly the images obtained from a variety of sensors--in order to acquire targets for the new generation of "brilliant weapons." Such capabilities also might be used at higher command levels for "situation assessments and planning aids."

Looking further into the twenty-first century, artificial intelligence could be linked with robotics to make possible completely unmanned aircraft, tanks, warships, and submarines. Such a development, of course, could well have a marked impact on the cost trade offs among different types of forces and on the evaluation of alternative military tactics and strategies. These technologies should not be expected to

influence operational inventories until the year
2020 or later, however, and in any case,counter
measures against these unmanned weapon systems, or
at least against the first generation of such
weapons, could be relatively easy to design.

Materials Technology. Developments in
materials technology also are having a significant
impact on the future security environment. The
use of advanced composite materials and ceramics
will make possible the deployment of lighter,
stronger, more durable, and less visible platforms
of all kinds, but particularly aircraft,
spacecraft, missiles, and submarines. The
development of "stealthy" platforms, which combine
advances in materials technology with other
technological developments, will greatly reduce
the detectability of aircraft and missiles and
perhaps other types of weapons within the next ten
years. Again, counter measures will reduce the
impact of this technological trend. Advances in
computing, for example, will probably make
possible the development of fire control systems
capable of tracking first-generation "stealth"
systems in the 1990s. Well into the next century
there will be a continuous competition between the
technology that suppresses the signals emitted by
various platforms and those advances in computing
that make possible the recognition of ever more
faint emissions.

Developments in materials technology also
will reduce U.S. and allied nations' dependence on
foreign sources of certain "strategic minerals."
One of the most enthusiastic respondents stated
that "The advanced countries should be much less
dependent on raw materials from less-developed
countries in twenty-five years than they are
today, if presently known material technologies
are fully exploited." A second respondent
predicted that accelerating applications of man
made materials will exert continual pressures on
the price of key raw materials, causing grave
economic problems for producer nations.

Space Technology. Advances in materials
technology are among several developments that

will make possible much greater exploitation of
space for military purposes. Within the next
twenty years, both the United States and the USSR
will be able to construct very large structures in
space at a relatively modest cost. Such
structures might make possible the deployment of
phased-array radars in space, which could be used
for the surveillance of oceans and land areas in
all kinds of weather and at night, as well as
during the day. Large optical structures also
might be erected in space, as could large antennas
for electronic intelligence. Manned space
stations would be another potential use of large
structures in space, but several respondents noted
that such stations would not be a development with
important security implications. In addition, the
potential use of nuclear power for directed energy
weapons, space-based radars, and space-based
battle management systems could facilitate the
military use of space.

   Directed Energy. Advances in space
technology could be linked with advances in
directed energy weapons to provide space-based
defensive systems, but the respondents to our
Delphi survey differed markedly in their
assessments of these prospects. Of those who
addressed this possibility, nearly all predicted
the development of effective anti-satellite
weapons (which would not necessarily be based in
space). Only a small minority forecast the
development of effective missile defenses within
the twenty year period of the study, however.
Among those who were optimistic concerning the
possibility of space-based, missile defense
systems, there were differing evaluations of such
a system's capabilities. Two argued that no
system could be more than 50 percent effective; a
third believed that "a low leakage" system was
feasible. Many asserted that even a limited
capability could not be expected given the
relative ease of countering any defensive systems.
If a weapon deployed in space were capable of
destroying offensive missiles, it also could
destroy the opponent's defensive system--hence a
stalemate.

Biotechnology. As noted previously, several respondents mentioned this area as one with potential impact on U.S. security interests, but they failed to specify how, exactly, that impact would be felt. One respondent noted that advances in biotechnology "certainly will affect our ability to fight disease and injury, and may well affect such matters as manufacturing processes so that it could in the longer run have an effect on our national security posture considered broadly." Most others were more vague:. For example,

> The most rapid scientific evolution occurring today is in biology, in particular the related fields of genetic engineering and immune mechanisms. It is difficult to foresee all the applications, but certainly the knowledge base and the capability to identify and activate specific agents will be very different in a decade or two from what it is now. I am only listing this development last because I do not have the imagination to see concretely the various security implications.

Potential applications of biotechnology that would have significant implications for military planning include the development of super lethal pathogens (and counters to super lethal pathogens), and improved and cheaper agricultural seed and medicines, both of which could measurably affect stability in the Third World.

Nuclear Technology. The development of pure fusion weapons a step that would lead to far more efficient weapon designs, could potentially have a major impact on U.S. and Soviet military capabilities within the next twenty years. The development of more compact weapons could have an adverse effect on U.S. security because such weapon systems could aggravate the threat of nuclear terrorism. The extension of nuclear technology to additional countries also could greatly increase the threats to U.S. security

(this potential development is discussed
separately below).

Specific Applications of New Technologies

The implications of the new technologies can
be described both on a functional basis and with
regard to specific weapon systems, as discussed in
the following sections.

Sensing. The development of more effective
sensing capabilities is probably the most
important potential application of advances in
computing technology. The ability to detect faint
signals of all kinds against cluttered (or noisy)
backgrounds will be combined with new
understandings of optics, infrared technology,
radar, lasers, and other sensing means to create--
by the turn of the century--both relatively small,
easily deployed sensors for tactical operations
and very large, space-based systems for a wider
range of purposes. Both developments will expand
military capabilities greatly. Target acquisition
systems that combine data from several types of
sensors (including some based in space) and
infrared surveillance systems are the most likely
applications of this technology.. Space-based
systems, it was maintained by one expert, "should
be able to detect almost anything of military
value on the ground." (These new sensing
capabilities will restrict the gains in
survivability otherwise to be expected from
"stealth" technology.) The greater distance
between sensors and their human interpreters made
feasible by the new technologies is particularly
significant. It would make possible the
development of "instrumented battlefields" before
the end of the century in which a variety of
acoustical, optical, infrared, radar, and laser-
scanning capabilities could be implanted in
regions of potential conflict long before the
outbreak of hostilities, thereby greatly enhancing
the capabilities of the defending side. This
development obviously would be of great importance

for such U.S. allies as West Germany and South
Korea.

Major improvements in computing and sensor
technology could have dramatic effects on
antisubmarine capabilities as well. Five of the
respondents discussed this possibility, although
only one made a confident prediction of
substantial improvements "in the long-range
detection and localization of quiet submarines"--
in the U.S. case, by the year 2000; in the Soviet
case, by 2010. These advances will result from
the development of supercomputers, the deployment
of autonomous sensing arrays, and greater
knowledge of the physics of the oceans. Computing
capabilities that make it possible to integrate
large quantities of data from several types of
sources will be particularly important in the
expansion of anitsubmarine capabilities. Although
the greatest advances in antisubmarine
capabilities are likely to result from continued
progress in acoustical means of detection, it is
also possible that developments in the U.S.
ability to detect nonacoustical emissions from
submarines, "including hydroelectromagnetic
phenomena and various chemical and physical
perturbations in the state of the ocean induced by
the presence and motion of submarines will improve
these capabilities." A radical advance in either
acoustical or nonacoustical detection capabilities
could have major strategic implications because of
its potential effect on the survivability of
submarine-launched ballistic missiles.
Nevertheless, it should be remembered that
technological advances also will reduce the
strength of the various signals emitted by
submarines. The conclusion of most of the
respondents who addressed antisubmarine
capabilities was captured in this response:
"Although these potentially significant
technologies have been and are being pursued by
the major powers, there is no basis at present for
a confident prediction of a major breakthrough.
On the other hand, some not negligible
evolutionary improvements in ASW, both
conventional and novel, must be expected over the
next twenty-five years."

Guidance. Improvements in guidance technology also will have a significant impact on military capabilities. Infrared seekers for both air-to-air and surface-to-air weapons will be improved particularly, but generally speaking, relatively cheap, highly accurate guidance systems will become available for the full-range of weapon delivery vehicles. Most importantly, this development--combined with new sensor technologies--will make possible a new generation of brilliant weapons. A particularly intriguing possibility is that guidance systems will become so accurate within the next twenty years as to make strategic weapons armed with conventional ordnance an attractive option. As one respondent put it:

> Very accurate warhead delivery may be achievable within the next decade using signals from the Global Positioning System to update the guidance subsystems on board a variety of delivery means. The impact of this development could make the use of nonnuclear munitions attractive in many applications. That in turn may greatly affect negotiations on arms control and the use of space, as well as the overall strategic and tactical postures of both the U.S. and U.S.S.R.

Communications. Many of the technologies already mentioned also will contribute to more capable communications systems. These developments are emerging as much in the civilian sectors of the Western industrial nations as in their military sectors. (Even so, the Soviets do not appear to be very far behind in this area.) Developments in communications technology will provide inexpensive systems able to handle large amounts of data very rapidly. The new systems are expected to be much more resilient as well. Indeed, one respondent noted that new communications systems could be expected to survive attacks better than the forces themselves, with the partial exception of submarines. The

20

major impact of these developments will be on the conventional battlefield.

Command and Control. One commentator suggested that an important consequence of the new electronic technology would be the renewed capacity of battlefield commanders "to get back on top of the hill." Computers, remote sensors, and advanced communications systems, he pointed out, would enable commanders to see the tactical situation coherently, as a whole, thus facilitating analysis of the tactical situation, the formulation of effective strategies, and the timely direction of troops in the field. An analogy is provided by the Airborne Warning and Control System (AWACS), which already permits the air commander to perceive the entire air situation in a theater as a coherent whole. New electronic technology will provide similar capabilities to commanders of ground forces by the end of the century.

Electronic Warfare. At the same time, several respondents mentioned the possibility of major advances in electronic warfare capabilities on both sides. According to one, "Electronic warfare, in many guises, will make it extraordinarily difficult for anyone to use forces or operate systems without interference." In thinking about future force structures, a key issue for military planners is the likely relative balance between improvements in guidance, communications, targeting, and other types of systems that depend on the new electronics on the one hand and the simultaneous improvement in electronic warfare capabilities, on the other.

Brilliant Weapons. Both the United States and USSR can be expected to deploy extremely accurate, autonomously guided, all-weather munitions before the end of the century. The United States can be expected to have these weapons in the field by the early 1990s, the Soviets by the late 1990s. These second-generation, precision-guided munitions will be made possible by the previously mentioned advances in sensing, guidance, and communications. Many of these weapons can be clustered in a single delivery vehicle, thus reducing the price per unit of capability. Perhaps the most important implication of these emerging weapons will be an increase in antitank capabilities.

Cruise Missiles. Several respondents also singled out cruise missiles for special comment. Not only will very accurate, relatively inexpensive cruise missiles be available to the United States and the Soviet Union, but by the end of the century these capabilities are likely to have spread to many other nations. The impact of advanced cruise missile capabilities on naval warfare will be particularly important. Adding soon-to-be-available logic circuits plus new antijamming and all-weather homing capabilities to existing cruise missile capabilities should greatly enhance the firepower of highly mobile surface platforms and submarines and increase the risk to warships. As these capabilities proliferate, the flexibility of the great powers in considering military operations against smaller nations will decline.

Remotely Piloted Vehicles (RPVs). New technology also will increase the potential capabilities of RPVs in the context of the land battle. This potential will be exploited largely to obtain very accurate, timely information about the battlefield, thus making possible better battle management and control.

Microwave Generators. Finally, three respondents mentioned the likely appearance of high-power, microwave generators on both sides in the 1990s. These systems, utilizing millimeter-wave radar, would have a multiple shot capability and be useful as antisensor, antielectronic, and antipersonnel weapons.

ECONOMIC STRENGTH AND ECONOMIC DEPENDENCE

In a narrow sense, relative economic strength influences the strategic environment for military planning by determining the amount and character

of resources that the United States, the Soviet
Union, and their respective allies potentially can
devote to national security. However, economic
strength influences political/military relations,
and thus the strategic environment, in more
comprehensive ways as well.

The strength and vitality of the U.S. economy
provides this country with a great deal of
leverage in its dealings with other nations. As a
source of goods, services, capital, and
technology, and as a market for exports and a
source of opportunities for investments, no
economy in the world is the equal of the U.S.
economy. Consequently, most nations prefer to
maintain stable and cooperative relations with
this country and, within limits, will adapt their
behavior accordingly. Stable and cooperative
relations between the United States and foreign
governments encourage the U.S. private sector to
look to those nations for investment and trade
opportunities. At a minimum, an absence of
hostile relations allows the private sector to
conclude economic arrangements without undue
government restrictions. In the case of positive
relations, the U.S. government may encourage
private sector activity as well as support, in
some cases, direct economic assistance bilaterally
or through multilateral lending organizations.
Obviously, some nations (Cuba, for example) prefer
adversarial relations with the United States on
political or ideological grounds in spite of the
economic costs that may be incurred. Still, such
cases are exceptions; most often, the U.S. economy
is a tremendous asset in the U.S. political,
economic, and military relations with other
countries.

At the same time, the nation's economic
requirements often cause the United States to
compete with adversaries (and sometimes with
political allies) for influence with foreign
governments. Interdependence, by definition, cuts
both ways. To some extent, the U.S. economic
well-being is dependent on the actions of others.
We require markets for our goods and services and
sources for our energy and raw material

requirements, and we often benefit from foreign
sources of specific manufactured products or
components. The need to preserve these economic
relations in order to maintain our economic health
and vitality can sometimes constrain U.S. foreign
policy and limit the freedom of action of U.S.
decisionmakers, causing them to pursue policies
which they might not otherwise consider seriously.

Economic Strengths

Perhaps the single most important determinant
of the U.S. position in the world is the size and
strength of its economy. With only 5 percent of
the world's population, the United States accounts
for fully one-fourth of the sum of the entire
world's Gross National Products (GNPs). The U.S.
economy employs more than 100 million people and
generates a GNP in excess of $3 trillion. This is
one-third greater than the combined GNPs of
Canada, France, Germany, Italy, and the United
Kingdom. With the addition of Japan, the combined
GNPs of these six countries exceeds that of the
United States by only 10 percent.

Much has been made in recent years of the
declining economic dominance of the United States,
but this apparent trend has been exaggerated.
Except for brief periods during the mid-1970s and
early 1980s, economic growth in the United States
has been remarkably strong and consistent during
the entire postwar era. The average annual rate
of growth from 1960 through 1984 was 5.1 percent.
From 1976 through 1984 it averaged 3.3 percent.
Not only do these figures represent strong
economic growth in and of themselves, but they
compare favorably to the growth rates experienced
by other industrial nations.

The size of the U.S. economy, however, tells
only part of the story. The importance and
influence of the United States in world affairs
are further enhanced by the favorable U.S.
position in international commerce. Although the
United States trades extensively, thus strongly
influencing the well-being of other nations, the

United States itself is proportionately less
dependent on international trade. For example,
U.S. exports in 1984 amounted to about
$180 billion. This was more than the total for
any other country and accounted for more than 12
percent of the total value of world exports and 18
percent of the total exports of the Organization
for Economic Cooperation and Development (OECD)
countries. Even so, U.S. exports amounted to only
7 percent of the U.S. Gross Domestic Product
(GDP). (West Germany is the second largest
exporter in the world, 1984 exports totaled $140
billion and accounted for more than 26 percent of
the German GDP.) U.S. imports of $270 billion in
1984 were equivalent to about 18 percent of total
world imports, approximately one-fourth of OECD
imports, and were approximately as large as the
total imports of all the non-oil-exporting
developing countries. As with exports, moreover,
U.S. imports are less significant to this
country's economy than their size would suggest.
U.S. imports were less than 10 percent of the
country's GDP in 1984. (West German imports,
again the second largest, were $130 billion,
approximately 23 percent of the German GDP.)

The significance of these figures goes beyond
their demonstration of the sheer size of the U.S.
economy. Despite the central role of the U.S.
economy in world commerce, the data suggest that
the United States is much less dependent on
international trade than are other countries.
Partially as a result of this disparity, the
United States possesses both greater influence and
greater freedom of action than do most other
nations that are involved actively in
international trade. As will be seen in
Chapter 3, these relative advantages can result in
political leverage for the United States in
several regions of the globe.

Economic Projections

What does the economic future look like? The
projections of GNP prepared for this study are
intended solely to provide a crude, comparative

glimpse of what resources the United States, its chief adversary, and their respective allies could have at their disposal during the next two decades. We are not attempting to forecast economic growth rates. The purpose of the exercise is simply to explore what seem to be the likely bounds of currently evident economic trends.

The growth rates experienced during the 1960-1973 period represent the probable upper bound of economic growth for the United States, the Soviet Union, and their respective allies; this was a period of extraordinarily rapid economic development by historical standards. The lower bound GNP projection for the United States (and its allies) was obtained by taking the average annual growth rate for the relatively low growth period of 1975-1983. A 2.0 percent average annual growth rate, taken from Central Intelligence Agency (CIA) studies, was used as the lower bound for the Soviet Union (and the other Warsaw Pact countries). This 2 percent figure assumes that the Soviet economy will continue to be plagued by the problems that currently beset Soviet planners (see Chapter 3, below). This, however, is hardly the most pessimistic forecast that could be made. Many experts believe that the Soviet economy may soon enter a period of sustained zero, or even negative, growth.

Based on these bounds, the range of projected GNP for the United States alone in the year 2000 would be approximately $5.6-7.2 trillion in 1985 dollars (see Figure 2.1), while the Soviet Union's GNP will likely range between $2.9 and $3.8 trillion. Even in the worst case, therefore, the U.S. GNP would exceed the USSR's by nearly 50 percent. The Soviet Union's comparative disadvantage worsens appreciably when the economies of each side's allies are considered as well. Our baseline projections indicate that by the year 2000, the North Atlantic Treaty Organization (NATO) and Japan will have a lower bound GNP that is nearly twice as great as the upper bound GNP of the Warsaw Pact nations (Figure 2.2). In short, the U.S. economy seems likely to continue to out-produce the Soviet economy, and the economies of the United States and its allies together will dwarf the productive capabilities of members of the Warsaw Pact. In the long term, these projections have important implications for the relative political influence of the United States in world affairs, as well as for its relative military capabilities.

Implications of U.S. Economic Strength

There are four basic implications of the size and performance of the U.S. economy: Economic strength potentially can provide the United States with great influence around the world; economic strength provides the nation with the potential to devote substantial resources to defense; the United States is dependent upon specific countries or regions of the world for particular goods or markets important for the continued growth of the economy, a factor that can influence security policies; and in the long term, U.S. security will depend partly on the overall performance of the global economy. The first two factors, influence and the availability of resources for defense,

Figure 2.1. Range of Projected GNP: United States and USSR

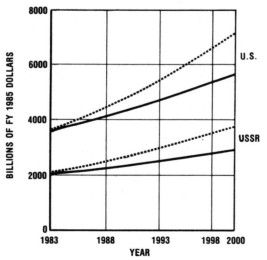

represent benefits that accrue to the United
States because of its strong economy. The second
two, dependencies on specific countries' specific
resources and on the long-term performance of the
global economy, reflect potential liabilities
incurred by the United States as a consequence of
its economic relations around the world.

    Influence. The economy is a fundamental
underpinning of the U.S. position in world
affairs. The actual, and even potential, impact
of our economic activity on the economic well-
being of other nations is an implicit element in
virtually all U.S. foreign relations. The
strength of the U.S. economy to a greater extent
than the nation's military power conditions other
nations' choices in their relations with the
United States on a day-to-day basis.

**Figure 2.2.   Range of Projected GNP:
NATO plus Japan and Warsaw Pact**

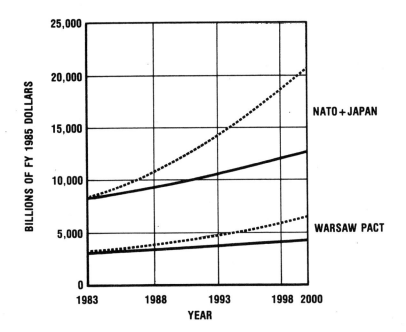

The economy's effects can be manifested in a
number of ways. The dynamism and relative success
of the U.S. economy causes it to be seen as a
model by government officials and private citizens
in countries throughout the globe; it is an
important component of the image that others hold
of us and reflects favorably on this country, its
values, and outlook. Particularly now that the
Soviet model of economic development has largely
been discredited, leaders of many Third World
nations are looking increasingly to the United
States for assistance in solving their own
economic problems. The evolution of relatively
cooperative relations with China during the past
ten years is a good example of this process, as is
the recent improvement in U.S. relations with
India. Similar effects can be seen among the
industrialized nations. The initial resurgence of
the U.S. economy following the recession of the
early 1980s had a notable impact on European
leaders and led to enhanced U. S. prestige and
influence abroad.

The size of the U.S. economy alone affects
the economic performance of other states. In the
early 1980s, for example, U.S. fiscal and monetary
policies leading to high interest rates attracted
considerable foreign capital to this country,
thereby diminishing the potential for economic
growth in European countries. At the same time,
these policies led to an overvalued U.S. dollar,
which encouraged exports to the United States from
Asia and other regions, just as it depleted the
foreign sales of U.S. manufacturing sectors.
Among the fragile economies of the Third World,
U.S. policies can have even more serious
repercussions. High U.S. interest rates were a
major contributor to the international debt crisis
in the early 1980s and its subsequent adverse
consequences in Latin American and African
economies.

Given the relationship between U.S. economic
policies and the economic stability of other
countries, foreign leaders sometimes seek to
influence domestic U.S. decisions--as in the

annual economic summits of the major industrial
powers. Theoretically, at least, this desire on
their part should give U.S. policy-makers leverage
in seeking other objectives. In the broadest
sense, the size of the U.S. economy means that,
all else being equal, foreign nations prefer to
have good relations with this country. In an
atmosphere of peaceful and cooperative relations,
foreigners can find markets for their products in
the United States and gain access to the advanced
technologies and other specialized goods and
expertise produced here and nowhere else. They
can also gain access to U.S. capital markets and
financial institutions. Such transnational
business transactions do not necessarily disappear
with the advent of difficult relations between
states, but business dealings can certainly be
made more difficult and far more risky in stressed
circumstances. It is particularly important for
states seeking private U.S. investments to create
stable relations with the nations around them;
investors have become chary of apparent
opportunities in unstable regions. This wariness
has potential advantage for U.S. policy-makers.

U.S. economic power also can be used in more
directed ways. Economic aid and technical
assistance can promote the effectiveness of
sympathetic governments, just as the denial of
such assistance can be, and often is used to
discredit hostile states. Bilateral aid and the
funds provided by multilateral lending
institutions, most of which are controlled by the
United States and its allies (as the key donors),
also can have the same function. Just in the past
few years, the overwhelming economic importance of
the United States to the entire Western
Hemisphere, especially to Central American and the
Caribbean nations, has been indicated quite
clearly. Relatively small amounts of economic
aid, by U.S. standards, have had far-reaching
positive effects (e.g., El Salvador), while
ostracization by the United States has resulted in
severe economic hardships (e.g., Cuba and
Nicaragua).

Conversely, the Soviet Union's apparent economic weakness clearly undercuts its global position and political influence. This was demonstrated in an unusually vivid way in southern Africa in 1984. At that time, Angola and Mozambique failed to receive commitments from the Soviet Union for the massive economic assistance they needed--presumably because the Soviets could not afford the cost of helping them. They were thus forced to reach accommodations with South Africa in order to establish a more stable environment in which greatly expanded U.S., West European, and multilateral investment and economic assistance would be made possible. The U.S. ability to offer economic aid was thus converted into political gains for the West and losses for the Soviets.

It is important to bear in mind that there are significant limits to the potential political influence to be derived from economic strength. Although economic sanctions imposed against Cuba have crippled the Cuban economy, they have not been successful in moderating Cuban behavior, as recent events in Central America, and prior to that, in Africa, attest to. Economic sanctions, in fact, have been notoriously ineffective, as post war experiences in Rhodesia, the Soviet Union, and Libya indicate. U.S. relations with the nations of East Asia are a more subtle illustration of the limits of economic influence. Currently, nearly one-fourth of Japan's exports are sold to the United States, while one-sixth of its imports came from the United States. The United States receives more than one-third of Korean and Philippine exports and supplies nearly one-fourth of their imports. Despite the clear economic importance of the U.S. to these nations, the ability of the United States to influence their policies, particularly domestic policies, has been distinctly circumscribed. The Japanese successfully resisted for many years U.S. demands for economic liberalization, as well as for significant increases in military expenditures. Similarly, political liberalization and reform in Korea has proceeded far more slowly than the United States has wished, despite U.S. economic dominance of the Korean economy. Events following the 1985 Aquino assassination in the Philippines, on the other hand, highlight the important role that the private sector of the economy can play in influencing events abroad. At least some of the movement toward political liberalization in the Philippines that followed Aquino's death and led eventually to the overthrow of President Marcos, can be attributed to pressures applied by foreign private economic interests.

Means of economic influence fall into two very general categories. The first form of influence is a result of trade and other private economic relations. The second is the result of official, government-to-government economic aid. Although less obvious, private sector activities are at least as powerful a form of influence as official aid, if not more so, by virtue of this sector's ability to generate commonalities of interest. Indeed, it may be the case that economic influence, although a poor means of achieving short-term objectives through directed government-sponsored means, may be the most important source of common interest and cooperative policies in the long-term.

Resources for Defense. The performance of the nation's economy constitutes a fundamental component of its national security. Economic growth expands the resource base available for military investment in peacetime and enhances the nation's industrial mobilization capacity in the event of war. A growing economy can ease the perceived burden of defense; thus military planners can argue more successfully for increased defense expenditures. When economic growth slows or turns negative, financing defense growth becomes more difficult, and public support for military expenditures usually declines. Our European allies appear to be particularly susceptible to such a relationship; when their economies have been troubled, as in recent years, the political consensus in each of those nations favoring substantial efforts for national security often has diminished.

Many factors determine the degree of a nation's support for defense expenditures, however. The state of the economy is far from the only, or even the primary determinant. During the early 1970s, a period of economic expansion, popular opinion in the United States strongly favored reductions in military expenditures. This contrasts markedly with the Reagan administration's initial defense buildup, which occurred during a severe economic recession. The public's perception of the threats to U.S. interests around the world may well be a more decisive determinant of the level of public support for arms expenditures than the performance of the economy. So, too, may be the public's perception that the burden of defense is being shared equally among the Western allies; a perception of unequal sacrifice also seems to lead to reduced support for defense expenditures. Nevertheless, there is a link in democratic nations--at least during peacetime--between economic well-being and the adequacy of resources made available for national defense. In this regard the United States possesses a great advantage by virtue of the size of its economy and because of its relatively promising outlook for sustained, if moderate, growth during the twenty year period of this forecast. In the following section, we describe the potential implications of the U.S. economic situation for future defense budgets and contrast them with those for the Soviet Union.

U.S. and Soviet Defense Resources. The projections of defense expenditures used here are based on a more eclectic set of trends than those employed for the previous projections of GNP. The highest real growth rate used in the projections for the United States (6.87 percent per year) reflects the pace of the defense buildup during fiscal years 1980-1984. This is probably an unrealistic figure in terms of sustained growth, but it can illustrate the conceivable upper bound of defense increases. The lowest U.S. baseline was constructed by assuming that the 1987-1991 defense program will be fulfilled as planned by the administration, followed by annual real increases of 1.0 percent to the year 2000. This averages out to a 3 percent compounded annual growth rate during the full period.

Two distinct periods stand out in the last twenty years of Soviet defense spending. CIA estimates suggest that from 1965 to 1976 there were steady, annual real increases of about 4.0 percent in Soviet defense expenditures. In 1977, however, the rate of increase in Soviet military spending slowed to 1.7 percent and remained at that annual rate through 1985. These two figures, 4.0 and 1.7 percent, are used to bound projections of future Soviet defense spending.

Experience during the high growth rate period of 1961-1980 was selected as the upper bound for the defense growth rate of the U.S. allies in Europe and Japan. This twenty year period saw considerable economic growth in all these countries and a generally stable governing consensus that made possible steady annual increases in defense expenditures. For NATO countries other than the United States, the high-range growth rate is 4.0 percent, and for Japan 11.0 percent. For the members of the Warsaw Pact other than the USSR, the comparable period of sustained economic growth and rising defense expenditures was 1966-1976: the average annual growth during this period was 7.3 percent, and this figure is used to project the high-range growth rate in defense expenditures.

Recent economic and political developments in Western Europe suggest that support for defense spending could continue to decline. Accordingly, the low-range growth rate assumed for members of NATO other than the United States is flat--that is, no growth. The period 1976-1983 (with a 0.8 percent growth rate) coincides with an economic downturn in Eastern Europe and was chosen for the low-range forecast for members of the Warsaw Pact other than the USSR.

Were the United States to resume increasing defense expenditures at the rate it did between 1980 and 1984, by the year 2000 the United States would be committing approximately 11.0 percent of

34

its projected mid-range GNP to defense
(Figure 2.3). If the USSR also pursued a defense
buildup at its highest plausible rate, the United
States would still be out spending the Soviet
Union by almost 30 percent. Nevertheless, the

**Figure 2.3. Range of Projected Military
Expenditures: United States and USSR**

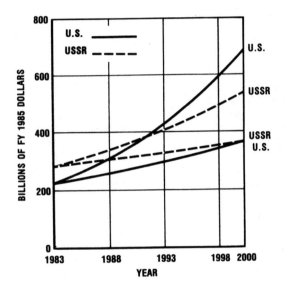

Soviet Union would be committing 16.2 percent of
its projected mid-range GNP to defense. In a
competition, not only would the Soviets be unable
to match U.S. defense expenditures, but also the
burden of defense on the Soviet economy would be
very great, much greater than that in the United
States.

If the United States and Soviet Union were to
follow their respective low-range growth trends,
on the other hand, their expenditures would be
comparable in absolute terms. They both would be
allocating approximately $365 billion (in 1985
dollars) to defense by the year 2000. However,

these figures represent only 5.7 percent of the
projected U.S. economy, but 11.1 percent of the
projected Soviet GNP--again a comparison that
greatly favors the United States.   When each
nation's allies are added to the equation, the
Soviet position worsens appreciably. A comparison
of projected defense expenditures for the two
alliances reveals that, at the high end, the
Western nations could be spending almost $1
trillion on defense annually by the year 2000 and
yet only be committing 5.8 percent of their
combined GNP (Figure 2.4). The Warsaw Pact could
reach an annual expenditure of approximately $650
billion, only two-thirds the Western total, yet
this would correspond to a burden of 13.0 percent
of their combined GNPs.

     The low-range projections for the West show
annual expenditures rising from close to $350
billion in 1985 dollars to $500 billion in the
year 2000.   This increase, however, would
represent a fall in the defense share of GNP from
4.2 percent to 2.9 percent. Comparable Warsaw
Pact low-range projections rise from $320 billion,
or 10.8 percent of GNP, to $420 billion, or 7.9
percent of GNP, in the year 2000. To match NATO's
low-range expenditures in the year 2000, the
Warsaw Pact would have to increase defense
expenditures at an annual rate of 2.6 percent. To
match NATO's high-range expenditures, it would
have to increase defense spending by an average of
6.9 percent each year and by the year 2000 would
spend fully 18.7 percent of its mid-range GNP on
national security.

     In an optimistic scenario, European members
of NATO would meet the alliance's aim of 3 percent
annual growth in defense expenditures.   If the
mid-range projections for the U.S. and Japan were
added to this figure, then total defense spending
by the West could reach $760 billion annually by
the year 2000.   This level of spending would
correspond to only 4.5 percent of the West's
combined, projected mid-range GNP.   In such an
eventuality, the Warsaw Pact would have to sustain
annual increases of 5.3 percent to match the West,
an effort that would require the Pact to commit

14.5 percent of its combined mid-range GNPs--a commitment nearly three times greater, in terms of available resources, than that of the West.

Figure 2.4. **Range of Projected Military Expenditures: NATO plus Japan and Warsaw Pact**

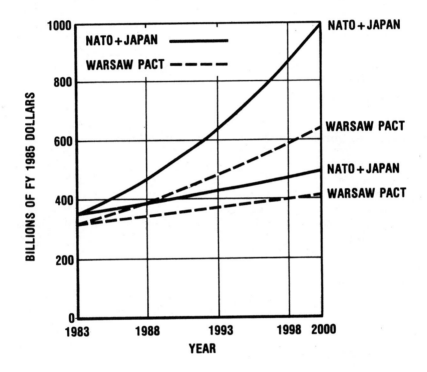

These are no more than parametric exercises. The data are strictly illustrative and, in any event, authoritarian governments like those of the Warsaw Pact nations are far more capable of sustaining heavy defense burdens in peacetime than are democratic nations. Still, the point is clear: The economies of the United States and other Western countries represent significant potential advantages in the continuing competition with the USSR.

Dependencies

Because of its trade and other economic relations around the world, the United States cannot help but become somewhat dependent on other nations for its economic well-being. These dependencies are of two types. The first consists of product dependencies, the reliance both on imports and exports of finished or semifinished manufactured products and services. The second, and perhaps more obvious, is resource dependencies--namely, dependencies on energy and minerals. Nevertheless, relative to most other industrialized countries, the U.S. economy's dependence upon exports and imports is small. Still, this dependence on foreign markets has increased substantially since 1970 (see Table 2.1).

TABLE 2.1.
Trade as a Percent of GDP

Nation	1970 Exports	Imports	1984 Exports	Imports
United States	4	4	7	10
West Germany	19	16	26	23
Japan	10	9	15	12
Canada	20	17	27	23
France	13	14	18	20
United Kingdom	16	18	21	21

In 1984, U.S. exports and imports were equivalent to 7 and 10 percent of the U.S. GDP respectively. Japan's exports and imports represented 27 percent of its GDP, followed by France, the U.K., Canada, and, finally, West Germany, whose exports accounted for 26 percent of GDP and whose imports were equivalent to 23 percent of GDP. Every country in the sample became more dependent on trade between 1970 and

1984, but the United States experienced the greatest increase in its relative dependence on foreign trade. In 1970, exports and imports each amounted to only 4 percent of GDP, almost one-half the 1984 figure. Approximately one-half of the increase in the value of imports between 1970 and 1984 can be attributed to energy imports, particularly to the higher price of petroleum.

The extent to which the U.S. economy became more interdependent with the economies of other countries and regions of the world is further evidenced in Tables 2.2 and 2.3. Note, for example, that in 1970 more than 63 percent of U.S. imports came from Europe and North America; only 27 percent came from Asia and Africa. By 1982, only 50 percent of U.S. imports were coming from Europe and North America, while more than 42 percent came from Asia and Africa. The figures for East and Southeast Asia are particularly noteworthy, and illustrate the rapid growth experienced by many of the countries in that region.

In 1981, 13.4 percent of U.S. manufacturing output and 12.8 percent of manufacturing employment relied directly or indirectly on exports. This represented a substantial portion of U.S. economic activity, and any diminution of international trade under these circumstances certainly would have had adverse effects on segments of the U.S. economy. This is precisely what happened from 1980 to 1982, when foreign trade contributed to one-third of the decline experienced in U.S. manufacturing employment during the economic recession of that period. The reasons for the decline in exports were quite simple. The steep appreciation of the U.S. dollar caused U.S. exporters to experience a severe price disadvantage on international markets and economic reccession among U.S. trading partners resulted in a lower demand for U.S. exports.

Table 2.2.
Destinations of U.S. Exports, 1970-1982
(Percentage of total U.S. Exports by region and country)

Region or Country	1970	1975	1980	1982
Developed countries	69.1	60.2	59.3	53.7
Developing countries	30.0	37.1	36.7	38.9
Communist areas	0.8	2.9	3.4	3.1
Africa	3.7	4.6	4.1.	4.8
Asia	23.2	26.2	27.3	2.7
Oceania	2.8	2.2	2.2	2.7
Europe	34.3	30.4	30.6	28.3
North America	28.6	28.0	25.7	24.5
South America	7.5	8.2	7.9	7.2
Western Hemisphere	**36.1**	**36.1**	**33.6**	**31.7**
Mexico	3.9	4.8	6.9	5.6
Venezuela	1.8	2.1	2.1	2.5
Brazil	1.9	2.8	2.0	1.6
Western Europe	**33.5**	**27.8**	**30.6**	**28.3**
Germany	6.3	4.8	5.0	4.4
U.K.	5.9	4.2	5.7	5.0
France	3.4	2.8	3.4	3.3
Near East	**3.1**	**7.7**	**5.4**	**7.5**
Saudi Arabia	0.3	1.4	2.6	4.3
Israel	1.4	1.4	0.9	1.1
Africa	**3.7**	**4.6**	**4.1**	**4.8**
Egypt	0.2	0.6	0.8	1.4
Nigeria	0.3	0.5	0.5	0.6
Algeria	0.1	0.6	0.2	0.4
South Africa	1.3	1.2	1.1	1.1
East & Southeast Asia	**9.3**	**9.4**	**10.7**	**11.8**
Taiwan	1.2	1.5	2.0	2.1
Hong Kong	0.9	0.8	1.2	1.2
Indonesia	0.6	0.8	0.7	1.0
Korea	1.5	1.6	2.1	2.6
Philippines	0.9	0.8	0.9	0.9
Singapore	0.6	0.9	1.4	1.5

Source: United States, Department of Commerce, Statistical Abstract of the United States, 1984 (Washington, D.C.: GPO, 1985).

Table 2.3.
Sources of U.S. Imports, 1970-1982
Percentage of total U.S. Imports by region and country

Region or Country	1970	1975	1980	1982
Developed countries	73.2	58.5	51.2	58.0
Developing countries	26.1	40.6	47.8	40.6
Communist areas	0.6	0.9	1.0	1.4
Africa	2.8	8.6	14.1	7.3
Asia	24.1	28.1	32.8	34.9
Oceania	2.2	1.6	1.4	1.3
Europe	28.5	22.3	19.0	21.5
North America	35.0	32.0	26.3	28.7
South America	7.4	7.5	5.9	5.9
Western Hemisphere	**42.4**	**39.4**	**32.1**	**34.6**
Mexico	3.1	3.2	5.1	6.4
Venezuela	2.7	3.7	2.2	2.0
Brazil	1.7	1.5	1.5	1.8
Western Europe	**28.0**	**21.6**	**19.0**	**21.5**
Germany	7.8	5.6	4.8	4.9
U.K.	5.5	3.9	4.0	5.4
France	2.4	2.2	2.2	2.3
Near East	**0.9**	**5.6**	**7.6**	**4.8**
Saudi Arabia	0.1	2.7	5.2	3.1
Israel	0.4	0.3	5.2	3.1
Africa	**2.8**	**8.6**	**14.1**	**7.3**
Egypt	0.1	---	0.2	0.2
Nigeria	0.2	3.4	4.5	2.9
Algeria	---	1.4	2.7	1.1
South Africa	0.7	0.9	1.4	0.8
East & Southeast Asia	**8.5**	**10.6**	**12.2**	**13.7**
Taiwan	1.4	2.0	2.8	3.6
Hong Kong	2.4	1.6	2.9	2.3
Indonesia	0.5	2.3	2.1	1.7
Korea	0.9	1.5	1.7	2.3
Philippines	1.2	0.6	1.7	2.3
Singapore	0.2	0.6	0.8	0.9

Source: United States, Department of Commerce, Statistical Abstract of the United States, 1984 (Washington, D.C.: GPO, 1985).

U.S. reliance on imports is more difficult to analyse quantitatively. (Here we are still considering products and services only, not energy and raw materials.) Given tremendous size and diversity of the U.S. economy, few products are imported that are not, or could not, also be manufactured here in great quantities. There is, for example, no foreign equivalent to the worldwide U.S. dominance in the aerospace and computer markets. Although many domestic industries have suffered in recent years from inroads made by foreign producers, none of these inroads presages either foreign domination of key U.S. industries or significant reliance on foreign sources of supply in any one industry. The "deindustrialization of America" was a myth spawned primarily by the despair of economic recession, a myth that has been easily refuted by recent research. Manufacturing as a whole has been an important agent of both economic growth and exports since the early 1970s and is expected to continue playing a central role in the years ahead. This does not mean, however, that specific industries within the manufacturing sector will not be faced with severe import competition. But even in those industries most severely affected (e.g., steel, autos, machine tools), there is rarely any suggestion that imports will make the U.S. completely or overly dependent on foreign sources of supply.

Foreign Sources of Petroleum. The importance of imported oil in U.S. energy consumption, the dramatic impact on the economy of the oil price shocks of 1973-1974 and 1979-1980, and the continued potential instability of U.S. and allied nations' oil supplies are at the root of concerns about the strategic implications of dependence on foreign oil. The United States and all other industrial nations have developed technologies and lifestyles that depend heavily on petroleum. Industrialized nations shifted steadily toward oil in the postwar period, and since the mid-1960s imports have risen sharply. Oil is a unique and important fuel for a number of reasons. It plays an important role in virtually

42

all energy-consuming sectors of the economy. Air and surface transport are technologically dependent on liquid fuels, a reality with important implications for national defense. Oil has a very low substitution potential in the short run and only modest potential during a longer period of time. Additionally, oil, or more precisely imported oil, is a vital residual energy source. Oil imports are an essential reservoir from which the United States and other countries could draw in response to sudden changes in supply or demand. The oil crises of the 1970s demonstrated that the dependence of the industrialized nations on imported oil can be quite costly. The chronic instability afflicting many of the countries on whom Western nations rely for significant shares of their oil imports, the many conflicts among nations in the oil-producing regions, and the uncertain motives and influence on the world oil market of the Organization of Petroleum Exporting Countries (OPEC) make continued dependence on foreign sources an important security consider-ation for the United States and its allies.

(a) The Role of Oil Imports in U.S. Energy Consumption. From 1952 to 1977, the proportion of U.S. petroleum demand met by imported oil rose from virtually zero to near 50 percent. The volume of oil imports increased tenfold during the period from 1952 to 1977, rising from less than 1 million barrels/day in 1952 to almost 9 million at the close of the 1970s. U.S. oil imports grew almost 13 percent per year from 1969 to 1973 and, despite the doubling of real oil prices in 1973, began to decline significantly only after the second price doubling in 1979.

The decline in U.S. dependence on foreign oil has been even more rapid than the buildup in that dependence in the 1970s. As the price of petroleum increased, U.S. oil became more competitive. Moreover, consumers and industrial users began to institute extensive conservation measures and to find alternative economical sources of energy. Finally, the worldwide recession in the early 1980s, caused in part by the sharp rise in oil prices, bit deeply into consumption. The upshot has been a drastic drop in U.S. imports of foreign oil. At their peak in 1977, oil imports accounted for about one-fourth of total U.S. energy consumption and nearly one-half of total oil consumption. In 1984, foreign oil accounted for only 15 percent of energy consumption and less than one-third of total energy. Imported oil as a fraction of total U.S. energy needs is expected to stabilize between 10 and 15 percent during the 1990s and drop below 10 percent in the first decade of the next century (see Figure 2.5). This would enable the United States to play a more independent role in its policies toward oil producers than was deemed

Figure 2.5.   Percentage of U.S. Energy Demand Met by Oil and Oil Imports

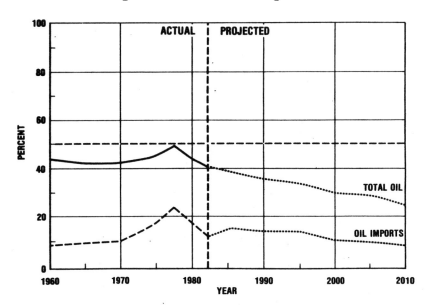

feasible ten years ago. Moreover, U.S. oil imports have been shifting from the unstable and politically sensitive Middle East to other sources. In 1977, nearly 40 percent of total U.S.

oil imports originated in nations bordering the
Persian Gulf--and an additional 10 percent came
from North Africa. In 1984, only 16 percent of
U.S. imports came from these two regions combined.
Mexico, Nigeria, and the United Kingdom have
become far more important as sources for U.S.
energy. (It was too early, at the time this
manuscript was set, to assess the impact of the
decline in oil prices in 1986. Presumably, if
these prices remain depressed, the trends toward
lower levels of imports will be modified.) The
change in the distribution of U.S. oil imports is
shown in Figure 2.6.

(b) Oil Imports in Western European and
Japanese Energy Consumption. Western Europe and
Japan rely on imported oil for their energy needs
to a much greater degree than does the United
States. Since the mid-1960s the nations of
Western Europe and Japan have imported between 80
and 100 percent of the petroleum they consumed.
During the 1970s, net petroleum imports provided
Western Europe with 60 percent of its total energy
requirements and Japan with 70 to 78 percent.
Following the oil price hikes of 1973-1974, Norway
and the United Kingdom were able to increase their
domestic production of oil and gradually lower
their dependence on imports, eventually becoming
net oil exporters by 1975 and 1980 respectively.
The other nations of Western Europe continue to
rely heavily on foreign oil, however.

Allied import dependence peaked at 70 percent
of total energy requirements in 1977-1978. Since
the second oil price shock and resulting
recession, Western European dependence on foreign
sources has declined and has been at less than
50 percent in recent years. Japan, like most
countries, responded to the oil price shocks with
fuel switching and conservation efforts but
achieved only minor reductions in its reliance on
foreign oil. The Japanese are making large
purchases of petroleum to fill a strategic
reserve, which would cushion the effects of a new
embargo or other disruption in supplies. European
nations have not taken any such steps.

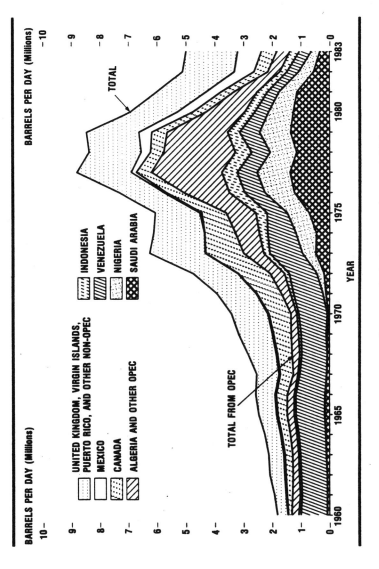

Source: U.S. Energy Information Administration, 1983 Annual Energy Review, (Washington, D.C.: GPO April 1984)

Figure 2.6.   U.S.   Imports   of   Petroleum   by   Country   of   Origin

46

The risk associated with allied dependence on
foreign oil derives not from the threat of
depletion of world reserves but from the potential
unreliability of supply. Oil reserves are
distributed with remarkable unevenness throughout
the earth, with nearly one-half located in the
countries of the Persian Gulf. Now, as in the
early 1970s, OPEC oil accounts for about
70 percent of the world's proven oil reserves and
about 80 percent of the total in noncommunist
countries. Persian Gulf crude oil production,
which made up about 30 percent of noncommunist
production in 1960, rose to a high of 50 percent
in 1977 before falling to its current level of
about 32 percent. OPEC's share of noncommunist
crude oil production increased from 45 percent in
1960 to 67 percent in 1977; it has since dropped
to about 50 percent as a result of increased non-
OPEC production and reduced Iranian exports.
Recently, Mexico has emerged as an important non-
OPEC supplier, with the fifth largest proven
reserves in the world. Most of the oil imported
by West European nations continues to originate in
Middle Eastern countries; Africa is Western
Europe's second largest source (Figure 2.7).
Japan, on the other hand, depends almost entirely
on Middle Eastern producers for its oil
(Figure 2.8).

Despite greater efficiency in energy use and
continued import reductions, Western Europe and
Japan can be expected to remain heavily dependent
on petroleum imports for their energy needs. In
fact, oil, imports are likely to increase as these
countries' economic growth gathers steam later in
the 1980s, particulary if oil prices remain
depressed. A U.S. Department of Energy study, for
example, projected declining shares of oil in
total primary energy consumption for all the OECD
countries, but Western European and Japanese
dependence on foreign oil was believed to be
unlikely to drop lower than 35 to 40 percent of
total energy demand through the year 2000
(Figure 2.9).

Figure 2.7.
The Role of Middle Eastern and African Oil in Total Western European Petroleum Consumption

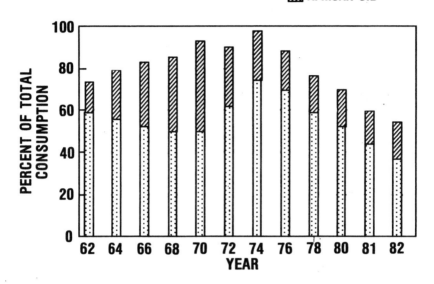

Source: American Petroleum Institute, Base Petroleum Data Book, Vol 3 (Washington, D.C., September 1983).

The risk of interuptions in oil supplies will thus continue to be a concern for the major U.S. allies. Of the individual producers, only Saudi Arabia could withhold supplies deliberately from the market with any effect. Apart from embargoes and other deliberate interruptions, however, sources of potential supply disruptions include the internal political, social, and economic stresses that have accompanied rapid modernization in the Persian Gulf and North Africa; interstate disputes, and terrorism. As in the case of higher oil prices, Western Europe and Japan would suffer

Figure 2.8. The Role of Middle Eastern and African Oil in Total Japanese Petroleum Consumption

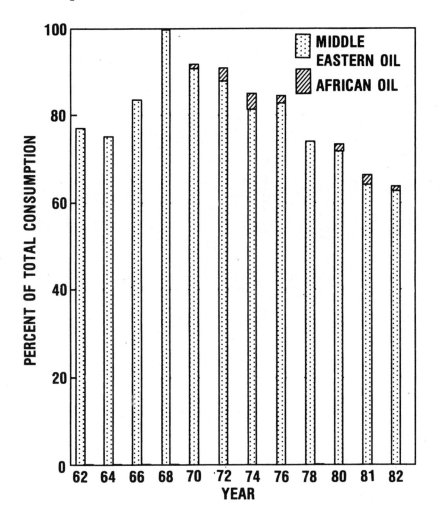

Source: American Petroleum Institute, <u>Basic Petroleum Data Book</u>, Vol 3 (Washington, D.C., September 1983).

far more from a sustained oil supply disruption
than would the United States. This is not
particularly comforting, however, as the economies
and political systems of the Western nations are
bound together so closely that the allies'
vulnerability represents a U.S. weakness as well.
The price increases that would accompany any oil
supply disruption would harm all the Western
economies, as would the coercive political power
that accrued to oil-producing nations should there
be an interruption in oil supplies.

Mineral Dependencies

The United States currently imports
75 percent or more of its requirements of twelve
nonfuel minerals (Figure 2.10). Of these, four
(chromium, cobalt, manganese, and platinum) are at
the center of concern regarding U.S. resource
dependencies; the bulk of these minerals are
supplied by insecure foreign sources, and each of
the four is important for the production of
weapons and other defense equipment. The United
States is 75 percent import-dependent for
chromium, and more than 90 percent import-
dependent for cobalt, manganese, and the platinum
group of metals. Although the United States
possesses large stockpiles of each of these
minerals, in the foreseeable future it will remain
particularly dependent on imports from the
Republic of South Africa and the USSR (chromium,
manganese, and platinum-group metals) and Zaire
and Zambia (cobalt). Other nations are able to
provide only minor amounts of each of these
minerals.

These dependencies must be taken into account
in U.S. military planning. However, these needs
should be placed in perspective when evaluating
their strategic implications. The value of all
U.S. nonfuel mineral imports is only a small
percentage of U.S. net expenditures on energy
acquired from abroad: only 5 percent in 1980, for
example. Between 1979 and 1981, the country's
annual net trade bill for nonfuel minerals

50

FIGURE 2.9. Oil as a Percentage of Western European and Japanese Energy Consumption

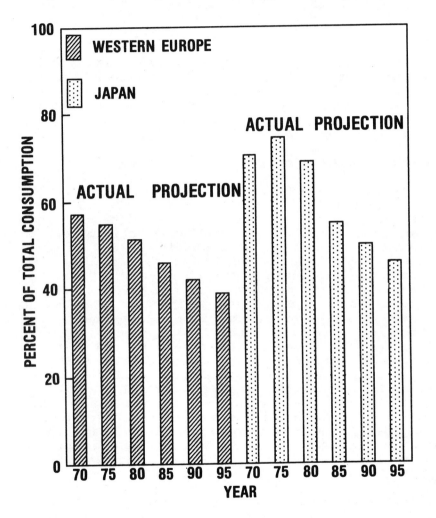

Source: American Petroleum Institute, Basic Petroleum Data Book, Vol 3 (Washington, D.C., September 1983)

51

Figure 2.10. U.S. Import Reliance for Strategic Minerals

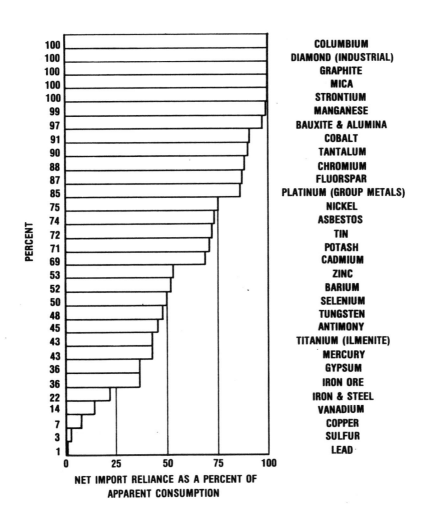

averaged only $6 billion. Furthermore, the four critical strategic minerals at the center of concern carry relatively low price tags--from $250 million to $500 million each annually, an amount equal in value to one to two days of imported petroleum. Supply disruptions of any of these materials would certainly be costly for the United States, but they would not have overwhelming economic consequences.

Although these minerals are necessary in essential industries, the quantities used are generally small, and most industries could accommodate price increases. When cobalt supplies from Zaire were disrupted in 1978-1979, for example, the result was a sharp rise in cobalt prices and some delays in the availability of key components. The industry hardest hit by this disruption was the jet engine industry, which utilizes cobalt in a number of key components. Even here, however, industry adjustments permitted continued production, only small increases in the price of engines, and no slippage in delivery schedules.

There are, nevertheless, specific risks involved in depending on foreign sources of strategic minerals. Potentially, producers could manipulate supplies, and thus prices, for political or economic gain. During a time of industrial mobilization for war, when demand would be rising sharply, disruption of production or transportation facilities could be a tactic employed by an adversary to good effect. During a war, alternative supply arrangements would probably have to be made. Many factors alleviate these potential problems, however. Producer cartels have proven ineffective in manipulating prices of nonfuel minerals, and the possibilities for alternative sources, conservation, and substitution appear to be quite extensive. Moreover, the economic needs of producers tend to be so great that they can ill afford the sacrifices necessary to withhold supplies for a period of time sufficient to make a substantial price gain. The existence of stockpiles of

strategic minerals in this country and in some
allied nations are an alternative to foreign
sources of supply should a disruption occur during
a war or crisis mobilization. So, too, is the
possibility of reinitiating domestic mining of
some strategic minerals. New extractive
technologies combined with rising prices could
make such domestic production economically
competitive in some cases.

Concerns about the national security
implications of import dependencies for strategic
minerals are likely to diminish in the next
century. Ceramics and man-made composite
materials are gaining wider applications.
Technologies are being developed that will permit
the exploitation of new sources of supply, and
industry is learning new means of conserving and
recycling critical commodities. Although the
nation's dependence on foreign sources of
strategic minerals implies some vulnerabilities,
these are small dangers compared to petroleum
dependencies and are likely to diminish further in
the future.

Global Political Economy

The strength and vitality of the U.S. economy
and its interdependencies with other economies
around the globe have additional implications for
political/military relationships and thus for the
strategic environment for U.S. military planning.

Many Americans believe that the sheer size of
the U.S. economy and the relatively high
proportion of the earth's resources consumed here
create a certain responsibility on the part of the
United States to provide economic assistance to
people in less fortunate nations and to help other
countries to develop economically. Those who
support this view understand the position as a
matter of ethics. Whether or not one subscribes
to such a viewpoint, it is clear that because many
Americans do take such a position, the flexibility
of U.S. foreign policy is constrained to some
degree. Funds allocated for the support of

bilateral or multilateral aid programs are not, of course, available for alternative uses. Moreover, U.S. attitudes toward particular countries in the poorest parts of the world--Central America, South Asia, and sub-Saharan Africa--and therefore U.S. policies toward those countries are colored by this particular senese of responsibility.

The strategic environment for military planning will be influenced by the rate of economic progress (or the lack thereof) in these poor regions in other ways as well. As will be made more explicit in Chapter 3, the increasing gap between rich and poor nations, falling or stagnant standards of living in parts of the globe, and rapidly rising populations create a political and economic climate that is potentially inimical to U.S. interests. It is difficult to predict the exact form this potential may take. In some cases, these pressures lead to massive migrations that give rise to regional instabilities and, if close to home, to tensions between the United States and the nation in question. Moreover, populations beset by economic failure, without any possiblity of self-advancement and living in squalor, particularly as compared to electronically conveyed images of life in the more advanced nations, are often recruiting grounds for terrorist organizations. The hopelessness and resentment bred in these regions are generally fertile soil for demagogues of all types. Their ideological labels may differ, but the message is the same. They urge violence, disorder, and radical change in place of peaceful and gradual transitions. As has been seen more than once in the postwar period, as in China in the 1940s and Egypt in the 1950s and 1960s, the results can have major effects on U.S. interests.

The strength of the U.S. economy carries with it broad responsibilities. Because it accounts for a substantial share of the world's total output and is the largest such share attributable to an individual nation, the United States has been, and will continue to be, thrust into a leadership position in the world economy, almost regardless of the relative degree of isolation preferred by its leaders and citizens. Desired or not, internal economic policy decisions affect-- sometimes pointedly--the economies of other nations. As was stated forcefully by Argentina's President Raoul Alfonsin in early 1984, to cite but one example, even small increases in U.S. interest rates can have drastic effects on the indebtedness problems of Latin American (and other) countries.

Given that the economies that are most interdependent with our own tend to be those of our closest political allies, it is particularly incumbent upon U.S. decisionmakers to consider international consequences in defining domestic U.S. policies. A failure to accept these responsibilities can affect political relation- ships adversely, and thus cooperation for security purposes. On the other hand, economic dependencies and responsibilities can develop into broader political/military commitments, or at least constrain the political/military choices available to U.S. decisionmakers. To the extent that the United States is economically dependent upon a specific nation, it often will seek to create an environment of cooperation with the country in question so that economic cooperation can be facilitated. At a minimum, the government will seek to avoid the development of hostile relations that might jeopardize favorable economic ties.

The U.S. relationship with Zaire is a good example of this dynamic. Were the strategic minerals the U.S. obtains from Zaire absent from the picture, Zaire would probably be the sort of nation with which we would prefer to remain at arms length, given that it has a somewhat capricious government that is generally considered corrupt and repressive. However, in the 1960s and early 1970s the United States sought to maintain favorable political relations with the Zairian government and in the process became closely allied with its leader, President Sese Mobutu, in order to avoid disruptions in Zaire's mineral exports. This association led in 1977 and 1978 to U.S. support for French/Belgian military

operations to defend the Zairian government from
an insurgent attack and to more direct forms of
U.S. military assistance to Zaire in the 1980s.
Less visible means of support also have been
provided and a fairly close political relationship
has evolved. By now, the United States is widely
perceived to have accepted a commitment to
preserve the Zairian government. Although this
perception may well prove to be false if it were
ever tested in conflict, for now its existence
colors political relations between the United
States and other nations in the region and thereby
influences the strategic environment for military
planning. In other words, the existence of
economic interdependencies often leads to the
maintenance of a political relationship in order
to facilitate economic cooperation. This
economically derived preference constrains foreign
policy choices and may even, at times, imply
security commitments that could eventually place
real demands on U.S. military resources. This is
one important way in which military commitments
are derived from the U.S. economy and its
interactions with the rest of the world.

NUCLEAR PROLIFERATION

The continuing proliferation of nuclear
capabilities shapes the future strategic
environment for several reasons. Nuclear weapons
pose the one clear threat to the physical security
of the United States. Thus, for many years, U.S.
policy has been based on the presumption that as
more nations possess nuclear weapons, the
likelihood of a nuclear war increases, as do the
risks to U.S. interests. Soviet decisionmakers
must have similar concerns, judging from the
USSR's relative cooperation in restraining the
spread of nuclear weapons to other nations.
Indeed, the majority of the most likely potential
proliferators tend to be adversaries of either the
USSR or a state supported by the USSR; threats to
Soviet interests implied by nuclear proliferation
may be greater than those perceived by U.S.
decisionmakers.

Many aspects of U.S. foreign policy--
particularly security commitments--are intended at
least in part to help persuade certain nations not
to seek a nuclear weapons capability; this
objective informs both U.S. policy toward the
potential proliferator and toward other nearby
nations. In the mid-1970s, for example, U.S.
policy toward East Asia was influenced by the
former's intention to persuade Taiwan and South
Korea to end (or at least reduce) what had been
substantial programs to achieve nuclear
capabilities. Once a nation acquires a nuclear
capability, moreover, particularly as its force of
operational weapons increases in size and becomes
more sophisticated, the fact of such capabilities
begins to influence the evolution of events in
that region, thereby potentially affecting U.S.
ties with a range of nations. Several analysts
have argued that such a process has occurred in
the Middle East since 1970--that the behavior of
Egypt and other nations is explained in large part
by their recognition of Israel's presumed nuclear
capabilities.

Therefore, the possibility that such hostile
nations as Iran or Libya may acquire nuclear
weapons must be factored into evaluations of
appropriate strategies and forces for several
contingencies. There may even be a risk of
nuclear terrorism, a risk that increases
substantially in the long term.

Forecasting the proliferation of nuclear
weapons is a twofold problem. The easier part is
to describe the facilities and other capabilities
necessary to build nuclear weapons, and to
identify the specific nations that may themselves
possess those physical capabilities or have access
to such facilities in other nations. This problem
is complicated by the convergences between
civilian nuclear power or research programs and
weapon manufacturing requirements, but these can
be dealt with relatively easily, particularly in
view of the international safeguards placed on
virtually all aspects of the nuclear fuel cycle by
most suppliers and recipients.

58

The more difficult aspect of forecasting proliferation is to identify which of this set of potential proliferators—those with the physical capacity to build weapons—actually would choose to exercise the option. This is a difficult decision for any state, as it requires a major investment of resources and, more importantly, can jeopardize both relations within a region and ties to external powers. Still, the benefits of acquiring a nuclear capability can be very important, particularly for those nations, like Israel or South Africa, that are relatively isolated in world affairs or, like India, that aspire to a larger world role.

Forecasts of the proliferation of nuclear weapon capabilities often have erred on the high side. In the mid-1960s, for example, many forecasts concluded that there would be twenty to thirty nuclear weapon states by 1990; however, most experts now expect one-third to one-half those numbers in the year 2000. Previous forecasts appear to have failed both on the intentions side of the problem, by underestimating the disincentives in acquiring nuclear capabilities, and on the capabilities side, by failing to foresee the relative effectiveness of the safeguards system erected by the international community.

The proliferation forecast used in this study was derived from a Delphi panel established specifically for this purpose. The methodology used to derive the proliferation forecast and the experts who constituted the panel are described in Appendix A. Suffice it to note here that the group was balanced between individuals with a technical background and those with a policy background, and between those who are very concerned about the possibility of nuclear proliferation and those who take a more relaxed view of these prospects. (There are some interesting contrasts between the views of the proliferation experts presented here and the predictions of the regional specialists inter-viewed for the forecasts of regional patterns of political/military relations; when appropriate, these contrasts are discussed in Chapters 3 and 4.)

The panelists were virtually unanimous in forecasting that India, Israel, and South Africa will have acquired a nuclear capability and, most believe, a substantial inventory of nuclear weapons before the end of the century. Indeed, several of the respondents believed that all three nations already have, or will very soon have, a small operational stock of weapons. Two of these nations have severe security problems and are relatively isolated in world affairs. The third aspires eventually to a leadership role in international politics. All three states have refused to ratify the Non-Proliferation Treaty and are known to have all the facilities necessary to manufacture nuclear weapons; these facilities are not, moreover, a part of the international safeguards prescribed by the Non-Proliferation Treaty.

The majority of the panelists predicted that five other nations will have acquired nuclear weapons before the end of the century. These five, in the order in which they are likely to acquire weapons, are: Pakistan, Brazil, Argentina, Taiwan, and South Korea. The first three countries are known to have active nuclear programs--allegedly for peaceful purposes--that will very soon provide them with complete (and unsafeguarded) systems that could be used to produce nuclear weapons. None of the three has signed the Non-Proliferation Treaty. Pakistan, in particular, is believed to be close to attaining a weapons capability and could test a nuclear device--putting it on a par with India--before the end of the decade. Taiwan and South Korea both maintained active nuclear programs at one time, and although both have since ratified the Non-Proliferation Treaty, given their security situations they may reconsider their positions. Additional potential proliferators include Japan, Iraq, Egypt, West Germany, Sweden, and Switzerland. The three European countries and Japan have advanced nuclear industries but little apparent incentive at present to develop an explicit weapons capability; these incentives might change, particularly for Japan. Both Iraq and Egypt, on the other hand, have expressed interest in acquiring nuclear weapons in the past but lack the technical capabilities. Egypt, at least, has since renounced such intentions, ratified the Non-Proliferation Treaty, and made arrangements to safeguard its nuclear facilities.

These forecasts are based on two assumptions about the future course of world events. First, no nuclear war will occur before the end of the century; any such conflict might greatly increase the likelihood of additional nuclear weapon states. Second, in the absence of U.S. security guarantees, an activist U.S. policy, and a forward military posture to make such guarantees credible, the likelihood of additional nuclear weapon states would increase substantially. Thus, between three and fourteen additional nuclear weapon states will be in place by the end of the century. In the most likely case, assuming that there is no nuclear war and that the United States continues to play an active role in world affairs, the actual number will be toward the lower end of the range, perhaps four to six (Israel, India, South Africa, Pakistan, possibly Brazil, and Argentina). This will be an important factor in U.S. military planning.

PUBLIC ATTITUDES TOWARD FOREIGN POLICY

In Chapter 3 of this book we discuss trends in political/military relationships in the several regions of the globe. The single most important factor shaping those trends is the behavior of the United States; specifically, the continued willingness of the United States to play an activist role in international politics. The likelihood that the United States will continue to play an aggressive role in world affairs, in turn, depends greatly on the attitudes of its citizens toward international relations and U.S. foreign policy. History has shown repeatedly that although the President (along with the Congress) has great latitude in formulating and implementing foreign policies, in the end those policies depend on the support of the U.S. public for their sustenance.

Although public attitudes toward the U.S. role in foreign affairs have varied widely during the years and can be differentiated greatly on the basis of specific issues, scholar and practitioners of the art of opinion analyses have identified certain underlying attitudes that seem to remain nearly constant. Two such basic attitudes are most relevant for the purposes of this study: The U.S. public broadly supports the maintenance of a "strong" military posture; the precise definition of "strong" varying in response to events and the position adopted by the President and other national leaders. Yet, there is a general reluctance among the population to become "involved" in the affairs of other nations, particularly when such involvement implies a risk of protracted military engagement.*

Military Strength

The U.S. public clearly understands the anarchic nature of the international political system and the essential role that military strength plays in assuring the nation's security within that system. The public generally supports policies--including budgetary allocations--to maintain the nation's strength for two reasons: deterrence, or as it is more commonly expressed, "to keep other nations from bothering us"; and defense, so that when the nation's interests are threatened directly, it has the capability to defend them. Obviously, the public's perception of what constitutes a necessary level of strength will vary. Support for increases in military strength diminishes following prolonged military buildups, just as it increases following periods of relatively low military spending. Perceptions

---

* This section draws heavily on an interview with, and the written work of, William Schneider. See, particularly, his "The Beleaguered Consensus," in Joseph S. Nye (ed.), Managing U.S.-Soviet Relations, New York: (Council on Foreign Relations, 1983).

of the need for greater defense efforts also vary
in response to events at home and abroad. Support
for military spending quite naturally diminishes
somewhat during periods of economic difficulties;
a growing economy, on the other hand, lends itself
to rising defense outlays. Support for military
buildups also is related to foreign events. The
loss of tangible interests abroad (e.g., seizure
of U.S. property), the "loss" of foreign leaders
or nations that had been friendly to this nation
(e.g., overthrow of Iran's shah), or perceived
insults to the nation's prestige or position
(e.g., riots in which U.S. symbols are desecrated)
all result in greater support for military
spending.

Most often, the public takes its cue from the
President. Presidential support for military
buildups is helpful in the budgetary process
itself, and but also ensures public support for
the program. When the president's preference runs
counter to the public's basic support for a
"strong" military posture, however, he can
sometimes be overruled. This occurred during the
Carter administration. During the first two years
of President Jimmy Carter's term, public opinion
consistently supported higher levels of military
spending than the president was proposing;
eventually, the administration altered its
position to fit the public's demands.

Public support for a "strong" military
posture is consistent and unlikely to change in
the future. Even when the public favors lower
levels of defense spending, that position is based
on a perception that in view of circumstances
(e.g., the economic situation, the international
situation) the nation's "strength" is sufficient.
Reduced public support for defense spending has
never been associated with a perception that
military "strength" was no longer important or
relevant.

However, in regard to support for nuclear
weapon programs, public opinion is mixed. At
present, the nuclear component of military
"strength" is often singled out by the public for

disapproval and generally receives less support than do improvements in conventional military capabilities. The public perceives nuclear weapons as special in character, which diminishes their utility and increases the risks associated with their potential use. The degree of public concern about nuclear weapons has varied; the current period is reminiscent of the late 1950s and very early 1960s. The public's concern about nuclear issues is qualitatively different than other "peace" issues, a concern that derives from the public's apocalyptic view of the consequences of nuclear war.

The antinuclear movement in the early 1980s, which attained considerable political importance, was indeed a grass roots movement in origin--its strength was evident before national political leaders began to associate themselves with it. The movement has been less evident in recent years, which reflects public approval of the president's commitment to negotiate controls on nuclear weapons and to build defenses capable of rendering them impotent and obsolete. What is not clear is whether a lack of progress toward these goals would diminish the strength of the antinuclear movement or whether the attitudes professed by the movement are likely to constitute a permanent factor in U.S. public opinion. This contrasts markedly with the situation in Europe, where the antinuclear movement appears to have become a permanent fixture of the political scene.

Involvement Abroad

There is a fundamental prejudice among the U.S. public against "involvement" in other countries' problems. This is a contemporary echo of traditional isolationist sentiments dating back to George Washington's warnings against foreign entanglements. The view of much of the U.S. population is that noninvolvement, particularly in relation to the deployment of troops, is the best guarantor of "peace." Combined with the maintenance of a "strong" military posture to deter others from involving themselves with U.S.

interests, noninvolvement, it is believed, will
protect the nation's security and interests. This
preference for military noninvolvement is not by
any means the result of the Vietnam experience; it
predates the U.S. military involvement in
Southeast Asia by centuries. However, the Vietnam
War did confirm what much of the public had long
suspected, which probably explains why popular
reaction against Vietnam and several subsequent
military involvements abroad (e.g., Salvador,
Lebanon) has been so powerful. In particular, the
Vietnam experience confirmed the public's basic
suspicion of the internationalist policies favored
by government experts and the foreign policy
elite. In its most basic terms, Vietnam confirmed
the popular view that if the "people" permit the
State Department, bureaucrats, and other "elites"
to have their way in foreign policy, the results
are likely to be catastrophic, and the price will
be paid not by those "elites" but by the general
public.

The U.S. population does not oppose all forms
of military involvement abroad. Swift, decisive
interventions almost always receive popular
support, particularly when the threat posed to
U.S. interests that necessitated the intervention
can be identified clearly. Retaliatory
operations, involving single airstrikes, for
example, generally receive overwhelming approval.
The contrast between the public's overwhelming
support for the 1983 Grenada operation and
continuing public pressures against proposed
small, but apparently open-ended, forms of
military involvement elsewhere in Central America
demonstrate the public's discrimination among
different forms of military intervention quite
vividly. Public opposition to military operations
that do not involve the deployment of ground
forces also tends to be less vocal, as the danger
of combat involvement is less pointed. This is
probably one reason why U.S. presidents have
tended to rely more on naval forces for crisis and
other "peacetime" operations; the political costs
of such military involvements are lower.

The U.S. public also has supported the deployment of substantial numbers of U.S. troops in Europe and East Asia for more than thirty years, support that deviates markedly from traditional U.S. attitudes. It should be noted, however, at least as concerns the European deployment, that the U.S. military presence originated as a deliberate, bipartisan initiative and has continued to receive the support of both major parties throughout the postwar period. Furthermore, the policy has not required the involvement of U.S. troops in combat, nor has the public perceived that there was any significant risk of combat. Nevertheless, public pressure to remove U.S. troops from Europe has occurred periodically. Indeed, given budgetory pressures in the late 1980s and growing perceptions of an undue U.S. defense "burden" relative to the allies, some reduction in the U.S. troop presence in Europe may be necessary during the next thirteen years if the basic U.S. policy toward Europe is to continue receiving popular support.

It is difficult to predict the future level of public support for policies necessitating U.S. military involvement abroad. On the one hand, support for internationalism tends to increase with educational level, which is rising across the nation. Moreover, the growing international interdependence of the U.S. economy is exposing U.S. businessmen and women, traditionally among the most isolationist elements of U.S. society, to less parochial experiences and a greater understanding of the benefits that attend an active U.S. role in world affairs. On the other hand, there is a growing belief that U.S. defense partnerships with Western Europe and nations in East Asia impose an extraordinary burden on the United States, a burden not shared equally by the treaty partners who, according to this view, are competing unfairly with U.S. industry for trade and other economic benefits. There has been a broad trend toward protectionism, reduced international cooperation, and even isolationism in many nations, a trend also in evidence in the United States.

The power of the traditional U.S. preference
for noninvolvement abroad remains strong,
particularly when such involvement is considered a
serious risk to U.S. lives. This attitude can be
overcome when the threat posed to U.S. interests
is clear, or it can be surmounted, in some cases,
by presidential leadership. An attitude of
noninvolvement, however, will continue to shape
the strategic environment for U.S. military
planning.

3

Regional Forecasts

The basis for U.S. military planning is determined primarily by evolving political and military relationships among nations, particularly as those relationships include the United States on the one hand, and the Soviet Union, on the other. These relationships, in turn, reflect various trends within each region--including demographics, social movements and attitudes, economic developments, and the spread of technologies--as well as the policies pursued by outside powers seeking to influence intraregional affairs. Currently, the relationships among the European nations and between those nations and the great powers place the greatest demands on U.S. military capabilities, but intraregional relations in Asia, Africa, and Latin America will be posing additional (or alternative) demands on U.S. military capabilities in the future.

There is no reliable, empirically-based model for forecasting the evolution of intraregional relationships; the precise means through which the determinants of intraregional relations interact with one another are dynamic, often quite subtle, and are therefore not amenable to accurate prediction. Usually economic determinants appear to be the dominant factor in international relations, but powerful social or religious movements, or simply the force of a charismatic leader, can move events in directions an economic analysis would never have predicted.

Given this absence of empirically-based models on which to base forecasts of intraregional political and military trends, there is little alternative but to rely on the intimate knowledge and implicit predictive models of academic and government experts. Each such expert will base his or her forecast on an unstated model of what is and what is not important in determining events in the particular region in question. These models will differ, sometimes significantly, which is a major drawback in the use of such opinion for the purpose of forecasting. Still, when a substantial number of experts are consulted, a consensus often emerges that can be accorded a certain amount of legitimacy and confidence.

The regional forecasts that follow are based primarily on interviews with sixty individuals, each of whom has had considerable experience either in the affairs of a particular region or in the broader questions of relations among nations. The interviews were structured, but the experts were encouraged to discuss whatever subjects they believed pertinent. Interviewees were promised nonattribution, and were offered the option of remaining anonymous, which only a few accepted.

The participants in these interviews included many individuals with experience at the highest levels of government--including a former secretary of state, two former secretaries of defense, a former national security adviser, a former chairman of the Joint Chiefs of Staff, and a former British foreign minister. The set of interviewees was balanced between individuals who have served in Republican and in Democratic administrations and between those who take a conservative view of world affairs and those whose views are more liberal. These balances were imposed both on the overall set of interviewees and on the subset for any one region. Some effort also was made to include within the group of interviewees a range of age groups and diverse backgrounds. There is a bias, however, toward individuals who have gained the pragmatic perspective associated with government service, a

fact that may have influenced the forecasts to
some extent.

Through these interviews, we sought to
identify for each region two de-scriptors. First,
based upon his or her perception of trends then
visible in the region, we asked each expert to
forecast the most likely pattern of
political/military relations during the next ten
to twenty years. These "surprise-free" forecasts
provide starting points for understanding how
trends in each region should influence U.S.
military planning. We then asked each expert to
describe less likely, but still plausible,
patterns of relations in each region. Thus, we
sought to identify the major uncer-tainties in the
region and particularly those uncertainties that
would pose the greatest risks to U.S. interests.
These uncertainties, or varia-tions of the
surprise-free forecast, provide the most important
means of constructing the alternative composite
strategic environments described in Chapter 4. In
this chapter we describe the surprise-free
forecasts and the major uncertainties for six
regions of the globe: Europe, the Soviet Union,
East and South Asia, the Middle East, sub-Saharan
Africa, and Latin America.

EUROPE

In a surprise-free scenario, the nations of
Europe would gain increasing autonomy from the
United States and the Soviet Union during the next
ten to twenty years. This trend will be evident
in both Eastern and Western Europe, but in neither
case will the shift toward greater autonomy be so
pronounced as to challenge either the current
basic alliance structure or the specific composition of NATO or the Warsaw Pact. In Eastern
Europe, the primary mobilizing political force
will continue to be nationalism. The persistent
strength of nationalistic appeals, despite forty
years of occupation by the Red Army, suggests that
this powerful motivator of events and opinions
will remain a fundamental determinant of national
behavior well into the next century. Poland, of

course, where an impressive underground infrastructure survived the military coup in 1982, is the most visible demonstration of the power of East European nationalism, but echoes of the Polish movement also can be seen in Czechoslovakia and East Germany. The economic independence shown by Hungary, the idiosyncratic foreign policy behavior of Rumania, and the East German efforts to build ties to the West are all further evidence of the power of East European nationalism. In the surprise-free forecast we thus expect continued strains within the Eastern bloc and constraints on the Soviet Union's ability to orchestrate internal developments.

The key question in contemplating the likely future course of events in Eastern Europe is what degree of diversity and autonomy Soviet leaders are likely to tolerate. By pursuing independence--whether in economic policy, internal political arrangements, or through various ties between themselves and the West--the East European countries are treading a dangerous line. At some point, Soviet leaders could feel compelled to intervene militarily in order to enforce a minimum degree of cohesion and stability among their erstwhile allies. Nevertheless, the Soviet Union is compelled to accept a greater degree of diversity within Eastern Europe and may indeed benefit from it to a degree.

As will be described shortly, the USSR's own economic prospects in the surprise-free forecast appear bleak; this means that fewer economic levers of coercion will be available to control East European countries. Soviet leaders will be reluctant to use force to control events outside their borders. In addition, the appearance of greater independence within the Warsaw Pact strengthens the appeal of detente and cooperative relations in Western Europe, thus improving the USSR's political standing, diminishing dependence on the United States, and facilitating beneficial economic relations; all are important Soviet objectives. The USSR's need to tolerate a greater degree of political and economic diversity within the Warsaw Pact is a relatively new factor with potentially important implications for U.S. military planning. As one of the most senior experts, speaking about dissent in Poland in the 1980s, remarked: "Old Joe Stalin would never have put up with the situation. In fact, he would have welcomed an opportunity to squash the Poles as a useful lesson to other Europeans. The new Soviet leaders may be getting soft."

As for Western Europe, in the surprise-free case there probably will be continued, but modest, economic growth and rising political strains, particularly between the nations of Europe and the United States. Political difficulties between the United States and its allies will arise largely as a reflection of real differences of interests between the two, but also might be tinged by a certain degree of anti-Americanism that grows from a negative reaction to U.S. culture and mores and a resentment of the greater wealth and power of the United States. U.S. interests will shift increasingly toward the Pacific during the remainder of the century, a result of the greater dynamism of Asian economies and the changing composition of the U.S. population. This trend could exacerbate the problems already in evidence in U.S.-European relations. However, these difficulties are unlikely to cause fundamental changes in NATO or the basic structure of relations in Europe, at least not in the surprise-free forecast. The alliance will most likely survive into the twenty-first century. It will not solve entirely the problems that have hampered the development of a fully effective defense posture in recent years; nor will its continued existence be called seriously into question.

The constraints on the alliance's defense posture now in evidence are likely to further hamper NATO's defense preparations in the future. These constraints include (1) Severe restrictions on increases in defense spending (there will be virtually no real growth in European defense budgets from 1985 through the 1990s); (2) powerful popular opposition against nuclear weapons, which will induce European governments to seek means of reducing reliance on nuclear threats in NATO's strategy; (3) a reluctance to move very far toward real integration of national military forces or toward national specialization along functional lines; and (4) increasing pressures (from this side of the Atlantic) for a reduction in the U.S. presence in Europe. On this latter point, virtually all the experts interviewed thought that if the size of the reduction was not excessive and if it were handled properly, a "substantial" withdrawal of U.S. forces would not necessarily have an adverse impact on U.S.-European defense cooperation.

These problems notwithstanding, the general consensus of the experts was that in the surprise-free scenario NATO would somehow "muddle through," making some improvements in conventional capabilities, some changes in its nuclear posture, and some modest progress toward greater standardization and interoperability. In no event would these improvements be nearly as great as Western security officials believe are necessary to build a robust defense posture, but they should be sufficient to maintain an effective deterrent in virtually all circumstances.

The major new development in the European political/military context is the increasing willingness of Germans on both sides of the border to emphasize the bonds of their common German identity. This greater attention to, and outspokenness about, a singular German heritage does not reflect a return to nineteenth century German nationalism. Germans on both sides of the border understand that there cannot be a reunified German state--at least not during the next twenty years. However, there is a greater common acknowledgment of the similarities in the German situations in East and West. Many Germans see themselves sharing common dangers--particularly in their dependence on the prudence and restraint of their respective great power allies to avoid nuclear war. Many Germans also see their countries as natural mediators between East and West.

This new emphasis in West Germany on the bond between both Germanies also represents a yearning for a stronger national identity, a trend associated primarily with the younger generations now assuming dominance in political life. Such aspirations are one factor leading to difficulties in the U.S.-German relationship, as more Germans recognize that U.S. and German interests are certainly compatible, but not necessarily identical. (Similar German impatience with unequal arrangements among European nations presage difficulties in West Germany's relations with other countries, particularly France.) The appearance in East Germany of this new attention to German identity is particularly noteworthy. However significant new official celebrations of historical German figures and events previously ignored by the East German government are, the most important effect of this trend has been to create additional channels of communications and exchanges between East and West, including some between private organizations and churches.

At present, the Soviet Union obviously is prepared to accept the emergence of special ties between the two Germanies only up to a point. The forced cancellation of East German leader Erich Honneker's planned visit to Bonn in September 1984 spoke volumes about the USSR's continued ability to circumscribe movement toward the new German identity. Nevertheless, the degree to which the Soviet Union already has accepted enriched ties between the Germanies is reflective of Soviet tolerance of East European nationalism. Soviet leaders are reluctant to intervene; they are preoccupied with their own internal problems, and they also perceive that there are benefits to be derived from closer intra-German ties in the form of indirect Soviet influence on West German politics and therefore on economic relations. How far this trend might go is uncertain. More than one-half of the experts believed that intra-German association cannot develop very much further, at least not in the near future, as it is "a very dangerous game for Honneker" and could lead to a Soviet crackdown. The trend also raises uneasy feelings among many in the West, particularly in France, where some see the new emphasis on German identity as a step toward a unified, neutralized German state.

The surprise-free projection of the future of Europe is thus relatively optimistic from a U.S. perspective and features continued dissension in Eastern Europe, relative tranquillity in Central Europe, and the continued ability of NATO to mount an adequate deterrent despite the well-known constraints on its options. There are three major uncertainties in this forecast, however, which, although unlikely, are plausible to varying degrees and would have major implications for U.S. military planning.

The first uncertainty is the most likely to occur: a new Soviet military intervention in Eastern Europe to enforce the authority of a regime expected to ensure closer conformity with Soviet policy and better control of a restive population. Poland is the most obvious scene of such an intervention, although it is far from the only potential target. Under a renewed and confident Soviet leadership, intervention probably becomes more likely. At the same time, a renewal of domestic discontent in Poland or another East European country could become more outspoken and perhaps violent before the end of the century, thereby causing Soviet leaders to act decisively.

The results of any new Soviet intervention in Eastern Europe are likely to be profound, although they would depend to some extent on how quickly and with how much violence the intervention were advanced. The probability that an attempt by the Red Army to suppress the Polish national movement would lead to widespread and intense violence is fairly high, and such a conflict would trigger uprisings elsewhere in Eastern Europe, including--according to a couple of the experts--the Soviet Union itself. Even if controlled quickly, however, an intervention in Eastern Europe most likely would lead to renewed West European attention to defense requirements and far greater cohesion within NATO. Just as the imposition of martial law in Poland seems to have resulted in a much tougher French posture toward the Soviet

Union, an overt military intervention could have comparable (and more exaggerated) results in Western Europe generally, including the demise of whatever nascent trend toward German neutralism may already exist.

The second uncertainty seems to be far less likely: the creation of a unified, neutralized, and, for all practical purposes, disarmed Germany. This possibility is the logical consequence of trends toward greater recognition of a common German identity and toward far richer ties between East and West Germany. Such a development, which envisions the detachment of both Germanies from their respective security alliances, obviously would have the most significant effects on U.S. military planning. At the same time, it would represent an extrapolation of current trends to a point well beyond that which most of the experts believed possible.

Several of those interviewed, however, saw the possibility of German reunification and neutralization as deeply rooted in economic and cultural factors. According to this view, West Germany is likely to become increasingly dependent upon East Germany and the remainder of the Eastern bloc for both markets and raw materials, a result of West Germany's less competitive (and technologically backward) position as compared to Japan, the United States, and certain other European countries. According to this view, German industries are not adapting to modern circumstances nearly as rapidly as those in other nations. At the same time, the Soviet Union and its allies are likely to find West Germany an increasingly important source of basic manufactured goods, capital, and other economic resources. As a result, West Germany will look increasingly to the East for its export markets, and the East will look increasingly toward West Germany for a variety of goods and economic services. These economic trends would naturally impart momentum to policies that support closer political ties and, perhaps, eventually reunification as well. Moreover, this theory continues, it is psychologically comforting for Germans to

drift closer to the East, as historically they
have always been much more a Central European
power than a part of the West. In a cultural
sense, a close alliance between France and Germany
or Britain and Germany is an unnatural one. Given
the history of the twentieth century, neutralization and effective demilitarization are
necessary for Germany to regain its complete
identity and resume its historic role in European
and world affairs.

The majority of the experts did not find this
argument persuasive, largely on economic grounds.
German respondents, particularly, found erroneous
the thesis that Germany will be unable to compete
effectively with other Western nations on a long-
term basis. They admitted to a technological lag
at present, but believed it would be short-lived.
There also was considerable skepticism that the
Soviet Union would ever permit a reunified
Germany, even under the conditions just specified.
Most believed that the USSR would never have
sufficient confidence in its ability to control
Germany politically and economically to permit
unification under any circumstances.

The odds that the third uncertainty would
ever become a reality depend largely on actions
taken by the United States. This variation
postulates the restructuring of NATO to exclude
the United States as a military member and the
emergence of an independent European military
alliance led implicitly by the French. Different
experts put forth different elaborations of this
possibility. In some, the United States would
remain associated with the new entity only in a
political sense--there might be cooperation on a
variety of issues but no common military planning.
In others, the United States might maintain a
residual nuclear commitment and, in still others,
also might commit seapower and airpower to the
defense of Europe. In all scenarios, however,
U.S. ground forces would be withdrawn totally from
Europe.

In all cases, moreover, the United States
would be supplanted as the primary Western power

in Europe--almost certainly as a result of its own decisions. Virtually all the respondents stated that an independent European defense entity could only come about as a result of a U.S. decision to withdraw all, or the most substantial portion of, U.S. forces from Europe. In such an event, Europeans would face the choice of seizing the initiative and maintaining an effective defense entity themselves or accepting a position in which they were effectively dominated by the Soviet Union. The success or failure of any independent European defense entity would depend crucially on France's willingness to "share" its nuclear capabilities--in effect, to replace the U.S. nuclear guarantees with its own. No other power could play this role, although the British certainly could contribute to some extent. All the experts agreed that the possibility of an independent German nuclear force is extremely farfetched. They disagreed on whether or not France might be willing to undertake the nuclear guarantor's role, even assuming that the United States had withdrawn from Europe. Some pointed to the greater cooperation in defense matters that has characterized recent French-German relations as evidence that such a relationship might be possible. Others argued that, in fact, the rhetoric of Franco-German defense cooperation has proceeded farther than its reality and that the French will never yield the one advantage they maintain over the Germans--their unilateral possession of nuclear capabilities.

THE SOVIET UNION

The experts consulted for this study painted a grim picture of the Soviet Union's prospects for the next ten to twenty years, disagreeing only in their relative degrees of pessimism. In the surprise-free forecast, the Soviet economy at best might turn around in the mid-1990s. But even this projection may be optimistic. In the surprise-free case, there is really little reason to expect the USSR to make significant progress toward the solution of its serious internal problems at any point during the next twenty years. This negative

outlook is based primarily on systemic problems in
the Soviet economy and form of government,
problems that have resulted in widespread societal
disaffection.   The Soviet government is not
nearing collapse by any means, nor is it even
threatened with serious instabilities, at least
not in the surprise-free case.   But widespread
recognition of the severity of the USSR's internal
difficulties is a key finding of this study with
important implications for the Soviet Union's
likely future posture in international affairs.

Planning cannot be based on surprise-free
forecasts alone, however.   It is important to
hedge against alternative developments, even if
they are unlikely to become realities.   Two such
uncertainties pertain to internal developments
within the USSR: the prospect that the new,
dynamic leadership of Mikhail Gorbachev could
implement the reforms necessary to break out of
the systemic limitations on Soviet economic
performance; and the alternate possibility that
systemic problems could become so severe as to
lead to serious disorders within the USSR.

Surprise-Free Forecast

The Soviet Union's primary internal problem
is a weak economy.   Soviet economic growth has
been slowing considerably for some years.
Estimates of future growth range from negative
rates to only modest real growth (1 or 2 percent
per year).   Even at the high end of this range,
the USSR probably would be losing additional
ground when compared to the economies of the
United States, most of its industrial allies, and
even some nations in Eastern Europe and the Third
World.   The Soviet Union's comparative position is
diminishing because of an apparent inability to
incorporate contemporary technologies in civilian
sectors, especially computer and other electronic
technologies.

The USSR's most pressing need is for
substantial capital investments to modernize its
economic infrastructure.   According to one of the

most pessimistic experts, "Even if military spending were frozen at present levels and consumption held constant, investment will decline in the future and the basis for economic growth will be eroded." The USSR's basic problem is that the devastation of the Soviet economy during World War II was so complete that during the first fifteen years of the postwar period, investment in almost any part of the infrastructure helped to create economic growth and explained the very rapid growth rates that were sustained even into the 1970s. The Soviet economy is now at the point, however, at which available capital must be targeted in order to improve productivity or to stimulate growth in other ways; however, the USSR's tight centralization and artificial pricing system preclude effective means of identifying the most important priorities.

There is no evidence that the Soviets are considering seriously the types of radical reforms necessary to break out of these systemic limitations--particularly decentralization and incentives for greater individual performance. (In effect, the Soviets must do what the Chinese have been doing recently.) Soviet planners did attempt such reforms, at least tentatively, in 1965 and in 1976, but in each case Communist party officials stepped in and reversed the measures that had been set in motion. This experience is a reminder that real economic reform will not occur without major changes in the Soviet political system as well.

Reforming the economic system in effect means denying the small elites that now benefit from current methods their advantageous positions--this would hit the party apparatchiks harder than any other group. In other words, there would have to be a real shift of political power, either away from the party to the military or security organs, or within the party to a younger, and perhaps more nationally minded, leadership cadre. Both are possibilities. Indeed, there does seem to be a generational shift taking place among Soviet officials, but the new apparatchiks appear no less interested in preserving power than did their predecessors.

Several experts cautioned against exaggerating the severity of the Soviet economic situation, particularly in regard to the possibility of radical change in the political system. "We are not dealing with a Soviet leadership so hard pressed that it is compelled either to cut a deal with the West or engage in adventures," one well-known expert stated. He added, however, that although he was confident of this assessment in the near term, his confidence declined as he looked out toward the end of the century. A few of the experts postulated the existence of considerable tension between the Soviet regime and the Russian people and even of a profound disaffection within Soviet society. Evidence of such alienation includes declining productivity and birthrates, soaring alcoholism and absenteeism, and so forth. These indicators are obviously interrelated and their meaning should not be exaggerated, but at least a substantial minority of the experts believed there is something fundamentally and observably wrong in Soviet society.

This disaffection most likely stems from increasing consumer unhappiness and a growing recognition of the difference between the quality of Soviet life and European life, to say nothing of life in the United States. In other words, whatever tension exists is more economic than political in origin. Nevertheless, during the late 1970s and early 1980s, under Leonid Brezhnev, Yuri Andropov, and Konstantin Chernenko, there was some evidence of growing disenchantment with the country's political leadership as well. Outspoken criticism of Chernenko by private Soviet citizens was reported frequently in the press--a most unusual development. Soviet political leaders seemed to be losing their legitimacy in the eyes of the people. As a consequence, the Soviet armed forces, which were, and are, revered and honored throughout Soviet society, achieved far greater prominence. The visible support of Soviet military officials confers a certain amount of respectability upon Soviet political leaders who, on their own, are perceived as largely corrupt and ineffectual.

The advent of Mikhail Gorbachev seems to have checked these trends, at least for a time. He is a popular leader, and his dynamic and charismatic style has given Soviet citizens a renewed source of pride. He also has instituted many new programs intended to squeeze greater productivity from the existing system; he has authorized some experimentation with modest reforms and has begun to make rapid changes in personnel, emphasizing honesty and effectiveness as the basis for personnel selection. These changes appear to have revived the legitimacy of the Soviet political system and may lead to some short-term gain in economic growth. They will not solve the fundamental problems in the Soviet economy, however, nor greatly improve the lot of the average consumer. Indeed, some measures aimed at increasing productivity will make life more difficult for Soviet citizens. Therefore, in the absence of more radical reforms, a renewal of the downturn in economic performance and the illegitimacy ascribed to the Soviet regime by its citizens may well occur before the end of the century and perhaps as early as 1990. In fact, given the raised expectations of Soviet citizens occasioned by Gorbachev's new style and associates, severe acceleration of the previous negative trends could result once it becomes evident that the system is not changing for the better.

In assessing future developments in the Soviet Union, the degree to which various nationalities might seek greater autonomy from the tight control currently exercised by the Russian-dominated central authorities is a significant variable. Asian nationalities within the USSR, at least for the remainder of this century, appear likely to remain quiescent. The many separate nationalities in central Asia have little sense of identity or nationhood--and little history of independent nationalism to draw on. There is no evidence that their Islamic identity presents a problem for the central Soviet authorities; as there are no signs of the spread of Islamic fundamentalism to the USSR. People in the southern Asian portions of the USSR seem relatively more content with their economic circumstances. The more moderate weather makes life somewhat easier and, by comparison with their previously primitive standard of living, the inhabitants of this part of the Soviet Union continue to benefit from the Soviet economic system.

However, toward the end of the century, one trend could cause difficulties in Asia. The relatively much higher population growth rates of the Asian minorities (the birthrate for Great Russians is below that necessary for zero growth) means increasing demands in these regions for meaningful jobs and other opportunities for advancement. If the Central Soviet authorities are not willing to satisfy these demands by reallocating resources to the regions now inhabited by Asian nationalities and are not able to persuade larger numbers of Central Asians to move to those regions of the Soviet Union planned for rapid development, there could be increasing unrest near the end of this century or the beginning of the next.

There were sharp differences among the experts as to the consequences of the nationalities problem within the Soviet armed forces. One analyst spoke of the creation of a secret society among the Russian officers to protect their interests in, and overwhelming dominance of, the officer corps--a development analogous to the secret Boer societies that protect the interests of officers of Dutch origin within South African institutions. Other experts discussed the difficulties the armed forces experience because of the limited education and modernity of Asian nationalities, and their resentment of Russian domination. But still others discounted these problems, and a few viewed Asian service in the armed forces as a positive experience that tends to socialize Asians as citizens of the USSR rather than as members of specific nationalities.

In the near term, the most difficult nationalities problems are likely to occur in the European portions of the USSR, particularly in the Ukraine and the Baltic states. Unrest in these regions is fed by nationalistic expressions in Eastern Europe, and to a limited extent, one can see echoes of movements like Solidarity within the Soviet Union itself. The degree to which these problems will emerge is related to economic performance, but they are very close to the surface and, in the event of serious economic failure, could become visible very quickly.

The implications of the surprise-free forecast for U.S. military planning are discussed in Chapter 5. In general, however, trends in the USSR can be viewed positively in terms of U.S. interests. Under the conditions specified in the surprise-free forecast, the Soviet Union is likely to be less assertive and generally preoccupied with internal problems during the remainder of the century. Soviet leaders seem to be reevaluating the relative costs and benefits of an active stance in the Third World and seem more reluctant to take on additional commitments there (see the section on Africa). These leaders see themselves on the defensive in Europe, which is the result of continuing problems in Eastern Europe and the significant failure of their efforts to capitalize politically on the disarray in Western Europe. This is not to say that the Soviet Union will give ground voluntarily, turn isolationist, or fail to capitalize on situations in which it perceives an opportunity to enhance its interests or harm those of the West with little risk. It suggests simply that, in the words of one of the experts, "the West's bargaining position is stronger now than it has been in a decade, and if the U.S. can sustain a moderately assertive foreign and defense policy, it will likely remain strong."

Breakout from Systemic Limitations

As noted previously, it is certainly possible that during the next twenty years the Soviet Union

144138

will take the steps necessary to free itself from current systemic limitations. Mikhail Gorbachev has consolidated power relatively quickly. He could remain the preeminent Soviet leader for the remainder of the century and beyond, which is certainly sufficient time to design and implement major changes in the Soviet economy. Gorbachev will require the cooperation of the military to accomplish major reforms, but, if anything, the Soviet armed forces appear likely to encourage change, not restrain it. The success of any reforms will depend upon many factors, not least of which is luck. Weather is extremely important in determining the success or failure of Soviet agriculture and, with it, the Soviet economy overall. Soviet economic performance also would be helped by a permissive international environment. Although the government will allocate to the armed forces whatever resources it perceives necessary for the nation's security, under most circumstances Soviet leaders would prefer to restrain military spending; they recognize the consequences of the military burden for economic performance. A permissive international environment also would facilitate economic growth by making possible greater imports of capital and technology and perhaps reducing limitations on markets for Soviet exports. These economic needs, in fact, explain the apparent change in Soviet attitudes toward the Reagan administration and the current major drive for arms control agreements.

If the Soviet economy recovered, Soviet leaders would no doubt exercise a stronger hand in world affairs. There is little information on the foreign policy views of younger Soviet leaders, but they are likely to be somewhat more confident of the Soviet Union's power, having grown up with it and having been spared the traumas of the early decades of the Soviet state. One expert remarked that in the context of an improving Soviet economy and stable leadership, he would expect that "on the margin, Soviet leaders will be more eager to test the USSR's power in world politics." A second expert noted that the next generation of Soviet leaders is unlikely to be as quick to back

away from confrontations with the United States as
in the past. In short, in the event of a renewal
of Soviet economic growth and the solution of
political problems, a more assertive Soviet
foreign policy, if not a more aggressive one, is
the likely case.

Serious Internal Disorders

It is also possible, although unlikely, that
the USSR's economic and political problems will
get significantly worse, not better. Left uncor-
rected, the trends toward lower (perhaps negative)
economic growth, political paralysis, and societal
disaffection could lead to serious internal
disorders within this century. Soviet authorities
would probably be able to cope with any such
problems that developed, but the possibilities of
industrial sabotage, labor disorders, and even
food riots are conceivable, as are the emergence
of overt nationalistic movements in parts of the
European USSR.

In any such eventuality, the threat posed by
the Soviet Union to U.S. interests would be
greatly reduced. The experts were asked
explicitly whether they thought that desperate
internal problems might prompt Soviet leaders into
adventures abroad as a means of diverting
attention and inducing greater domestic cohesion.
The majority thought not, arguing that internal
problems greatly weakened the USSR's will and
ability to mount challenges abroad.

EAST AND SOUTH ASIA

Asia and the Pacific are clearly playing an
increasingly important role in U.S. foreign
policy, and the experts interviewed for this study
were virtually unanimous in predicting that this
trend will continue during the next twenty years.
They also forecasted a continuation of East and
South Asia's very impressive economic growth
throughout this period, at least in the surprise-
free scenario. Moreover, in the surprise-free

case, it was expected that the performance of the political systems of certain key nations will improve markedly and will result in greater political stability along with impressive economic performance. The experts' forecast for East and South Asia is the most optimistic of the six regional projections.

Three feasible developments could alter this prospect significantly. There is considerable uncertainty as to whether China can maintain the impressive economic growth, political stability, and pragmatic foreign and domestic policies that have characterized it since the late 1970s. The development of an unstable situation within China or a shift in Chinese policy toward alternative policies could have severe implications for U.S. military planning. Equally significant would be a major change in Japan's overall foreign policy orientation. There is some risk, although a very slim one, that during the next twenty years Japan will decide to pursue a more independent and assertive foreign policy, and build the sub-stantial conventional and even nuclear forces necessary to backup such a policy. This, too, would have major implications for U.S. defense planning. Finally, several of the countries on the rim of the Asian mainland--particularly India, Indonesia, and the Philippines--face severe internal problems that could lead to radical changes in government. The situation in Korea, also, must be considered unstable, although this potential instability grows from the possibility of a new war on the peninsula rather than from internal problems.

China. -- Under the leadership of Deng Xiaoping, China has instituted far-ranging political and economic reforms that have made possible sustained economic growth on the order of 6 percent per year. These reforms include decentralization and the intro-duction of incentives to encourage entrepre-neurship and high individual productivity. For example, some state revenues are remanded to local governments to spend on local projects according to their own priorities. Farmers are allowed to sell crops produced beyond established quotas on the open market. Individuals are permitted to open small businesses that employ others, and workers in some state enterprises are allowed to retain a portion of the profit from production beyond official quotas. In addition, the Chinese government has pursued the pragmatic foreign policies necessary to attract foreign investors, to gain access to foreign technology and expertise, and to obtain loans and development assistance from multinational organizations.

The experts we interviewed contended that in the most likely case the high rate of Chinese economic growth will continue for some years and average between 4 and 5 percent during the entire twenty-year period. With such growth rates, China could make substantial progress in raising the living standard of its people and developing a modern industrialized society. Much depends, however, on China's ability to control its population growth. Considerable progress has been made in this regard, but more so in the cities than in the countryside where three-fourths of the Chinese people live. Without further success in lowering the population growth rate (and also without continued good harvests--which means relatively good weather), much of China's pro-spective economic growth will be necessary simply to maintain the present living standard, a situation that could be conducive to renewed political instability. So far, in the country-side, China's economic growth has resulted in the creation of a small class of relatively rich peasants and modest improvements in the quality of life of the majority of people. If the promise of continued expansion of the class of relatively well-off people and further advances in the average standard of living are not continually fulfilled, resentments could grow and have adverse implications for political stability. Much also depends on China's ability to maintain favorable ties with Japan, the United States, and other industrialized democracies. The U.S. relationship is particularly dependent on how the Taiwan issue is handled--a sudden break in the current arrange-ment, perhaps a move by the Taiwanese to establish

Taiwan as an independent nation, would cause
severe difficulties for U.S.-China ties. So, too,
would a new war or even a confrontation in Korea.

In the surprise-free case, China's relations
with the Soviet Union are not expected to change
substantially. Both nations will attempt to
improve the tone of the relationship and avoid
conflict, but China has little incentive to seek a
more far-reaching accommodation with the USSR.
Although the two are bound to some degree by their
common obeisance to Marxist-Leninist ideology,
their differences--in terms of territorial disputes, very real racial hostilities, and even the
proper interpretation of Communist theory in
contemporary circumstances--are far more significant. Sino-Soviet ties also will be influenced by
relations between China and Vietnam. One expert
projected that China will be even less
accommodating as far as Vietnam is concerned in
the future; he believed that a real bitterness has
entered that relationship. So long as China
remains relatively weak militarily, as is expected
for at least ten more years, there is little to be
gained from this enmity, except base rights in
Southeast Asia for the USSR. But in the long run,
this expert, at least, would not be surprised if
China acted to settle old scores.

There is considerable concern about what
might happen after the death of Deng Xiaoping. He
is the last Chinese official with roots in, and
good ties with, the three key institutions in
Chinese life--the party, the government, and the
armed services. He is also the last prominent
survivor of the Long March, which confers on him
additional prestige and influence. It is conceivable that following Deng's death a struggle
may ensue among the three institutions for
dominance and between those who favor the
pragmatic policies established by Deng and those
who might wish to return to more ideologically
orthodox policies, such as those implanted in
China by the Soviet Union in the 1950s. The armed
forces also might bid for a larger share of the
political (and resource) pie in such a situation.
Modernization of the Chinese armed forces has been

delayed substantially in recent years, a situation about which the military leadership is becoming increasingly restive.

The net outcome of such a tumultuous situation is difficult to forecast. Much would depend on how much time Deng had had to pursue current policies and to place individuals with similar ideas in key positions. There clearly are struggles within the Chinese ruling establishment, as suggested by the various campaigns on cultural and ideological issues that have proceeded in fits and starts in recent years. There could be an orderly succession following Deng's demise and a new leader who continued to pursue the same pragmatic policies; or there could simply be a period of prolonged instability in which various forces struggled for control in different parts of the country. Eventually, power might be seized by a faction--perhaps in the armed forces--that had become dependent upon Soviet support and favored a return to more orthodox, highly centralized economic and political systems, with the resulting development of closer ties between the two nations. Or the military might take over on its own and establish, according to one expert, relatively autonomous military governments on a provincial basis. One option that was ruled out by most of the experts was a return to the ideological fervor of the Cultural Revolution. The excesses of that period apparently have thoroughly discredited the more extreme interpretations of Maoist thought.

Should Deng die in the near future, the balance of domestic forces in Beijing could be influenced strongly by U.S. and Soviet policies toward the region. Pro-Soviet factions could be greatly assisted by either a determined Soviet effort to bring peace to Southeast Asia and reach accommodation with the PRC in Central Asia or by U.S. policies toward the Taiwan issue or Korea that forced China's hand. A continuation of recent U.S. policies toward the region, on the other hand, benefits those who would continue Deng's reforms.

Japan. -- Developments in China also will be influenced by directions in Japanese foreign policy. One expert emphasized that the Chinese are made nervous by Japanese rearmament plans, even within the current parameters, and that this causes China to seek closer ties with the United States as a means of gaining some influence on Japanese plans. Accelerated Japanese rearmament, however, par-ticularly if it occurred along with a U.S.-Japanese split, could cause severe reactions in China. These tensions arise largely for historical reasons and will diminish as a new generation of Chinese come to power, but are likely to persist at least through the end of the century.

In the surprise-free case, Japan will continue to experience substantial economic growth based increasingly on high technology industries, to remain stable politically, and to adopt gradually a more assertive foreign policy within the framework of the security relationship with the United States. As such, the military capabilities of the Japanese armed forces will rise slowly, but not so much as to cause real concern in neighboring states or to provoke the Soviet Union. Japanese-Soviet ties are projected to remain correct, but very cool. None of the experts foresaw either a settlement of the Northern Territories controversy, the conclusion of a Soviet Japanese peace treaty, or a signifi-cant expansion of trade and other economic interactions between the two countries.

A sharp increase in Japanese rearmament could have a severe impact on China and its policies, regardless of the policy context in which such an increase occurred. Several experts postulated that at some point during the forecast period, following some catalytic event such as a U.S. failure to respond to a crisis in Korea or the Persian Gulf or the development of sharper Japanese-U.S. trade conflicts, Japan could move away from the United States and pursue a more independent foreign policy. Serious pursuit of such a course could lead eventually to termination of the U.S.-Japan Security Treaty, the withdrawal of U.S. forces from Japan, and a substantial expansion of the Japanese armed forces. With a solid industrial base already in place in Japan, it would be relatively easy for the Japanese to acquire powerful, modern armed forces rapidly once a decision to invest substantial financial, personnel and other resources required to expand the size of the Japanese military services was made. When queried the experts agreed that even the development of an independent Japanese nuclear force was conceivable, but all thought such a possibility extremely remote during the next twenty years.

Even without a nuclear component, however, the development of substantial Japanese armed forces in pursuit of an independent and more assertive foreign policy would have the most serious consequences for the political/military environment in East Asia. It could well drive China back into the arms of the Soviet Union and create a very unstable situation between both those countries and Japan. One or the other, or both, could attempt to force the unification of Korea under a friendly regime, thus preempting any Japanese attempt to reextend its former dominance of the peninsula. There could be considerable tension throughout the region if the nations of Southeast Asia also reacted with renewed fears of Japanese domination. If the Japanese decided to rearm significantly beyond current plans but did so while remaining in the U.S.-Japan security relationship and in conformance with U.S. policies, the consequences would be less radical but might still lead to instabilities in the region. China's reaction, particularly, is hard to predict; much would depend on the balance of power in Beijing at the time. The nations of Southeast Asia would not like the development, but their responses could probably be moderated by U.S. and Japanese assurances. The Soviet Union almost certainly would react strongly, although it is not clear in what way. Various contingencies

involving Korea would have to be considered, among
other possible adverse developments.

Asian rimland. -- The political stability
of several countries on the rim of the region
constitutes another crucial uncertainty. In the
surprise-free forecast, these nations (India,
Indonesia, Korea, and the Philippines) are
generally expected to continue recording
impressive economic growth rates and to move
increasingly toward stable political systems--the
usual concomitant of sustained, moderate economic
growth. There is some danger, however, of serious
political unrest and disorders in some of these
countries. India is the largest of these problem
countries and suffers from chronic unrest among
various ethnic and religious groups demanding
greater autonomy, if not outright independence.
Although none of these movements is that serious
at present, if the Indian economy were to suffer a
serious setback, there could be substantial
pressures for the effective dismemberment of the
Indian nation.

In Indonesia and Korea the problem is more
political; unpopular regimes perceived by many to
be corrupt and repressive maintain tenuous holds
on authority and could be overthrown at any point
during the period. Korea's internal political
unrest has persisted despite efforts of the Chun
regime to control corruption in government and to
initiate a modicum of political reform that might
lead eventually to the reemergence of democratic
practices.

Any forecast of Asian events also must
consider the possibility of a new war in Korea.
Again, this is primarily a near-term problem.
According to many of the experts, North Korea
believes that there now exists a window of
opportunity that will close as South Korea's
remarkable economic growth increasingly overwhelms
the North's capabilities. An overt invasion is
very unlikely given the presence of U.S. troops;
there is a possibility, however, of renewed
northern subversion and terrorism in the South
leading to military clashes and eventually to a

new war. Such a campaign might even be encouraged by the Soviet Union if it adopted a more aggressive policy toward the region--in response, for instance, to a sudden and significant increase in Japanese rearmament. Internal unrest in South Korea stemming from political difficulties also could encourage the North to step up attempts to subvert the government in Seoul.

In Southeast Asia, Vietnam's continued occupation of Cambodia and the resulting guerrilla war in that nation constitute the primary uncertainty. This conflict at times results in border incidents involving Thai forces. Although unlikely, the possibility of escalation to a broader regional conflict cannot be ruled out. In the Philippines, internal problems have eased in the near term as a result of Corazon Aquino's accession to power, but the country's basic problems persist. The communist insurgency continues and is aided by severe economic problems in the rural areas. Armed uprisings by Muslim insurgents complicate the situation. A violent revolution in the Philippines of course would threaten the important U.S. bases there.

The strategic environment in East and South Asia will continue to be dominated by relations between the United States and China on the one hand and between China and the Soviet Union on the other. Relations between Japan and each of the first three powers also will have a significant effect. Although developments in other nations could influence these great power relationships and affect their security positions in specific ways (e.g., by denying base rights), in terms of military planning, relations among the great powers are the crucial variables.

THE MIDDLE EAST

The forecast for the Middle East (including both North Africa and Southwest Asia) is surprisingly optimistic given the tremendous conflict and upheaval in the region during the past forty years. Projections of Middle East developments must be carefully hedged, however, and, even the experts seemed to have less confidence in forecasting future trends in this region than in any other.

In effect, there is an unstable balance of two contending social forces in the region. One force, which is modernistic in its direction, incorporates secular, pragmatic, and moderate elements. The second force, which stems from traditional roots, comprises religious, idealistic, and ideological elements. On balance, it appears that the struggle between these contending forces is being won slowly by the modernist tendency. The contest is far from over, however, and the balance could swing perceptibly in response to events. Interestingly, the experts believed that in the long run the outcome will be determined largely by the nations of the region, with the great powers playing only marginal roles. Egypt is probably the swing state in the struggle--the one in which the conflict is drawn most tightly and that will have the most profound effect on neighboring countries. Egypt's position is of particular import for U.S. military planning.

The rate and distribution of economic development are likely to be the crucial determinants of the course of events. There are large masses of people in the region, particularly in the cities, with virtually no connection to organized, secular society, no economic opportunity, and no hope for their own futures. These people tend to be young (more than 50 percent are less than twenty years of age) and far better informed about the world and their relative deprivation--thanks to modern communications--than their counterparts were even twenty-five years ago. This is the breeding ground for extremist ideologies--whether religious or secular in origin--that promise escape from present futilities and the achievement of idealistic objectives. The same class of people that provided support for pan-Arab nationalism and leaders like Egypt's Gamal Abdel Nasser in the 1950s and 1960s now forms the basis for

fundamentalist religious movements and the radical
policies, such as terrorism, that those movements
sometimes espouse.

The primary question is can the economies of
the Middle Eastern countries grow fast enough (and
can population growth can be contained
sufficiently) to offer significantly greater
opportunity and better living conditions for the
region's populations, thus reducing the appeal of
extremist movements. Can key governments implement domestic policies that open up the political
processes in their countries somewhat and give
their disaffected citizens a sense of participation in government and a stake in maintaining
the existing system? In fact, are the moderate
governments of the region, together with the
United States and other external supporters,
capable of pursuing policies that can defuse
potential international conflicts, thus avoiding
the emergence of new, and the exacerbation of old,
"causes" that attract the support of the
impoverished classes and thus provide openings for
extremists?

The experts' hesitant answer to these
questions was a qualified yes, and thus the
surprise-free forecast envisions the gradual
moderation of conflict within the region and a
slow evolution toward sustained economic growth
and political stability. This is not to suggest
that there will not continue to be both
international and domestic violence in the Middle
East throughout the remainder of the century, even
in the surprise-free case. This scenario simply
implies that we may have seen the worst of the
region's conflicts already and that the future
trend will be toward greater internal stability
and the peaceful resolution of external disputes.
Several factors support this assessment:

1. There has been continued economic
   growth in most countries leading to a
   slow expansion of a middle class with
   a stake in stability, rising educational levels, and the gradual

extension of secular and modernist perspectives.

2. There is growing recognition within the region that the Iranian revolution has failed and therefore constitutes a diminished threat to other governments. The Khomeini government has shown itself to be not only more brutal than the government of the shah, but also move incompetent, "incapable of either ruling or of defeating the Iraqis, by war or revolution."

3. There are recent signs that greater popular participation in domestic political systems is being encouraged by moderate governments. Jordan, for example, revived its Parliament in early 1984; this is one of the few national outlets for political participation by Palestinians. In addition, Egypt held elections in May 1984 that were less tarnished by manipulation than any since the 1960s. They resulted in the election of a genuine opposition party to a substantial number of seats in the Egyptian Parliament, a party that can provide a voice within the system for individuals opposed to the government's policies. In several other states, governments are permitting more open dissent and encouraging discussions of future moves toward more broadly based political participation and even democratic rule.

4. An alliance of moderate, pro-Western governments able to cooperate to a far greater extent than in the past, including Egypt, Jordan, Saudi Arabia, Iraq, and moderate Palestinian factions, appears to be emerging. These governments--which take a pragmatic view of world affairs--tend to be pro-

Western largely because of economic
considerations, but also because of
their fears of the Soviet Union.

Assuming that these trends persist, the next
twenty years are likely to witness the gradual
amelioration of conflicts in the region and
continued progress toward greater stability both
within national political systems, and between
governments. In the words of one expert, the most
likely case would see:

> progress toward Arab-Israeli peace--no
> utopian settlement, but progress in fits
> and starts; the building of a moderate
> Arab coalition that cooperates quietly
> with Israel, and continued progress
> toward closer cooperation among the
> members of the Gulf Cooperation Council,
> the gradual erosion of traditional
> regimes through a broadening of their
> systems of government, the downfall of
> the Iranian Mullahs following their chal-
> lenge by the Iranian middle class and
> armed forces

Arab-Israeli Conflict

A formal settlement of this forty-year-old
conflict is unlikely. It is possible, however,
that the conflict will "slowly wither away," with
Arab governments less and less willing to support
the Palestinians militarily and more willing to
cooperate quietly with Israel for various
purposes. This forecast depends not only on the
continued viability of relatively moderate regimes
in Egypt and Jordan, but also on the continuance
of governments in Israel able and willing to
facilitate such cooperative behavior. Such a
forecast does not exclude additional violence
between Israel and Arab governments. Indeed,
several of the experts forecasted a new Israeli-
Syrian war before the end of the 1980s, but also
argued that such a conflict would be necessary
for, and would make possible, a tacit settlement
of differences between the two states. As for the

Palestinians, the experts suggested that either
they eventually will supplant the Hashemites as
the dominant force in Jordan or that some sort of
"fuzzy" settlement will be reached that in effect
creates a Palestinian entity of some sort on the
West Bank without actually stating that this is
what had been done.

Iran-Iraq Conflict

There is unlikely to be a formal or
definitive settlement of the Iran-Iraq conflict.
Although there might be prolonged truces or quiet
periods, in the absence of a change of regimes the
war seems likely to continue for a long time--"for
a generation," several experts said--with neither
party able to win a decisive victory. If there
were to be a change of regime, the experts
hesitantly forecasted that it would more likely
take place in Iran than in Iraq, but that such a
change would not auger a return to a pro-Western
government. A new Iranian government probably
would incorporate religious elements under the
leadership of a fiercely nationalistic, military
regime. Attaturk's regime in Turkey earlier in
this century exemplifies the model.

Other Gulf States

A very positive element in the past ten years
has been demonstrated by the Saudi government's
considerable stability despite difficult events
and domestic pressures. There is little reason to
expect this situation to change. There will be a
generational break in the royal family by the end
of the century, after which there would be no
automatically logical successor to the king, no
precedent for succession, and therefore the
potential for a power struggle. Conflict among
the members of the royal family at this point
could lead to, and perhaps necessitate a greater
role for other elements in the Saudi government--
such as the army and the technocrats--and
therefore an uncertain situation.

The future robustness of the oil market of
course will play an important role in determining
the stability of all the Gulf states. In this
sense, the current disarray in the market and a
precipitous decline in the price of oil could have
some long-term negative consequences for U.S.
interests. The effects are less likely to be felt
in the major oil-producing countries, which have
very substantial reserves, than in those
neighboring nations that have benefited indirectly
from oil revenues. Egypt, for example, depends
importantly on earnings sent home from Egyptian
nationals employed in Saudi Arabia and other Gulf
countries, and other governments, Jordan and Syria
in particular, have been the recipients of Saudi
economic and military assistance.

Influence of the Great Powers

Soviet actions in the Middle East in the
surprise-free forecast are likely to be limited to
a small arena. The USSR will continue to maintain
a strong position in Libya, South Yemen, and Syria
and might even pick up one additional client--
Kuwait was mentioned as a possibility by one of
the experts, but the Soviet Union can be expected
to have only limited influence and leverage on the
mainline Arab governments. On a popular level,
the influence of the USSR derives strictly from
its professed support for the Palestinian cause
and perhaps from some residual association with
the struggle against imperialism. On official
levels, Soviet influence derives mainly from the
USSR's provision of military aid and other
"security services" to embattled governments. At
the same time, the Soviet Union is understood to
have very little to offer the nations of the
Middle East in the way of economic assistance--the
real problem facing these governments--and nothing
to offer in the way of diplomatic leverage against
Israel. Moreover, the Soviet tendency to meddle
in the affairs of those governments that do accept
their help is well known and understood, and the
official atheism of the Soviet government is a
distinct hindrance in its relations with all
Middle Eastern states.

Overt U.S. influence will not be great either, although the tremendous leverage associated with the U.S. economy, particularly in the energy sector, assures a far broader role for this country than for the USSR. Our development assistance and role in multinational lending institutions, coupled with the investment capital and technical services offered by private U.S. firms are the primary determinants of an assured U.S. role in the region. Still, in the surprise-free case, these forms of leverage are insufficient to achieve a more prominent and decisive U.S. position in the region. Our experts thought it unlikely, for example, that the Gulf states would accept an overt U.S. military presence on their territories at any point in the next twenty years.

Key Uncertainties

There are two great risks in this otherwise optimistic forecast. First, one certainly cannot rule out the possibility that fundamentalist movements will reverse recent trends and gain control of additional, perhaps key, governments in the region. An Iranian victory in the Gulf war, for example, could greatly magnify the prospects for the eventual triumph of Khomeini-style forces in the smaller Gulf states and even, perhaps, in Saudi Arabia (or in parts of it). Similarly, the failure of the Egyptian government to manage its substantial internal problems effectively--perhaps because of uncontrollable events such as a natural calamity--could result in a violent revolution in that country and the establishment of a radical regime. Other governments considered particularly vulnerable to a fundamentalist revolution include Pakistan, the Sudan, and Tunisia. As shown in the most recent election, even Israel may be vulnerable to the accession of extremist governments that would make a pragmatic solution of the region's problems difficult--and the likelihood of a fundamentalist take-over of Egypt far greater. In terms of U.S. military planning, the most important implication of these contingencies would be enhanced threats of state-sponsored terrorism, severe risks to western economic interests, particularly oil supplies, and greater oppor- tunities for the enhancement of Soviet influence .

Second, the possibility of a reinvigorated Arab-Israeli conflict cannot be considered a remote contingency. A fundamentalist revolution in Egypt, of course, almost certainly would mean the return of that country to the ranks of the "confrontation states" (and Jordan along with it) and an eventual resumption of overt military conflict with Israel. But an escalation in the Arab-Israeli conflict could emerge even if key Arab nations continue to move toward moderate policies. In the event of a new Israeli-Syrian war, for example, there would be considerable pressure on the Egyptian government to intervene, depending upon the chain of events precipitating the conflict. Or, for that matter, greater Israeli pressure on the West Bank and Gaza--an official annexation, for example, combined with an accelerated and expanded settlements policy--could lead eventually to a reversal of Egypt's current policy of peaceful coexistence and the resumption of widespread Arab-Israeli violence. In terms of U.S. military planning, the most important impli- cations of a renewal of the Arab-Israeli conflict would be more limited access for U.S. forces to bases and staging and overflight rights in Arab nations; greater opportunities for Soviet involve- ment in the Middle East and, with them, greater access for Soviet armed forces to the region; and, in the long term, a risk that nuclear weapons might be used by one or more of the belligerents, a development with severe implications for the risk of U.S.-Soviet conflict.

SUB-SAHARAN AFRICA

Trends in Africa appear to be dominated by the overwhelming economic problems of the region. The most severe drought ever recorded has worsened significantly what was already an extremely serious situation in large portions of the continent. The results--mass malnutrition and even starvation in some areas, grinding poverty, only slow progress toward modernization in some sectors--dominate considerations of political advantage or disadvantage. There is little reason to expect progress toward the solution of Africa's overwhelming economic problems in the near term. "Perhaps things might get better in the 1990s," one expert suggested, "but certainly not for the remainder of this decade." A second expert was even more pessimistic and foresaw food riots in widespread urban areas in the near term and significant problems throughout the century.

These economic problems have clear political implications. In the 1980s alone, coups or attempted coups have taken place in Ghana, Guinea, Kenya, Liberia, Nigeria, Uganda, and Upper Volta, to say nothing of the continuing insurgencies in Angola, Chad, Lesotho, and Mozambique. The coups follow a common pattern; they are led by younger military officers expressing impatience with existing economic models, both Marxist and capitalist, which typically mask a high degree of corruption and incompetence. Each successful coup raises new expectations, but none has exhibited any considerable degree of success.

The stark economic needs and political instability of most African countries put strict limits on the flexibility of their governments. Only Western nations and Western-controlled multilateral lending institutions can provide the investment, technology, markets, and outright grant aid Africans need so desperately. Consequently, regardless of ideological preferences and personal beliefs, leaders of African states typically perceive little choice but to create conditions conducive to Western economic involvement.

This was demonstrated graphically in 1984 in the case of Angola and Mozambique. Both governments are ruled by regimes that profess Marxist-Leninist ideologies and were dependent upon Soviet and Cuban support as revolutionary movements. Angolan leaders remain dependent on Cuban troops for continued control of insurgent forces within their country. Both nations have experienced severe economic difficulties in recent years, in part because of the great drought and other inescapable circumstances, but also because of deliberate policies on the part of the South African government. South Africa has provided covert support for dissident, revolutionary movements in both countries and has pursued a policy of overt military actions on the territory of Angola and Mozambique aimed at disrupting anti-South African and Namibian guerrilla organizations. The resulting high level of violence and instability had a severe impact on economic activity in the southern portions of the two countries and also adversely affected the climate for Western investment in, and assistance to, Angola and Mozambique.

According to several of our experts, both governments sought relief from this situation by asking the Soviet Union to grant them status as members of the Soviet economic bloc, as had been granted previously to Cuba and Vietnam. The Soviets declined, apparently believing themselves to be too greatly extended already to assume these additional responsibilities. As a result, the two governments were forced to reach accommodation with South Africa on the latter's terms, thereby specifically committing themselves not to provide support to organizations seeking to overthrow the South African government.

Soviet influence in Africa is limited by other factors as well. The Soviets are known throughout Africa as racists, their racism is considered far more extreme then any practiced by the United States or even former colonial powers. They also are perceived as inveterate meddlers in the internal affairs of African nations. In country after country in Africa (Ghana, Guinea, Mali), the USSR has carved out an influential position for a while, but then has been requested to leave because of its heavy handed attempts to interfere in internal politics. These lessons have not been lost upon African leaders.

With regard to South Africa, neither an orderly transition nor a violent revolution should be expected; instead, the experts foresaw a gradually deteriorating internal situation involving greater, but still containable, violence. They believed that a real transfer of power to the black majority through peaceful means is virtually unimaginable. Some largely symbolic steps might be taken in that direction. There also might be a further accrual of power by black labor unions and other grass roots organizations, a trend that could ameliorate some of the worst aspects of black living conditions in South Africa. But no real transfer of political authority or change in the relative distribution of economic wealth is likely in that country. As a consequence, and particularly in view of the 1984 South African agreements with Angola and Mozambique and the more recent one with Lesotho, a younger, more radical, and more violence-prone leadership cadre eventually will take over the primary revolutionary organization, the African National Congress. One result of such a change would be a sharp increase in violent incidents. However, as one expert put it, "no one believes the revolution is at hand. The government's repressive powers are huge--and the fragmentation of black politics greatly weakens the prospects for successful revolution."

There will be continuing, and in some cases increasing, pressures for the breakup of some of the larger African nations. The colonial boundaries that still delineate modern African nations in many cases threw together ethnic groups with long histories of conflict in territories lacking any geographic, economic, or demographic impetus to national cohesion. Moreover, in most cases the colonial powers created neither an economic infrastructure nor the institutions necessary to build a nation. The analogy usually drawn is with India, which comprises a variety of ethnic and religious groupings. In the Indian case, however, the British did create a substantial economic infrastructure and also left a certain legacy of nationhood--in the armed forces and in a competent bureaucracy, among others. In the African case, the decolonization process was so much more rapid that virtually no infrastructure was created to hold many of these countries together, except for modest armed forces.

In addition to Chad and Uganda, which in effect have been divided for several years, the most severe problems are faced by Ethiopia, Zaire, Angola, and Nigeria. In Ethiopia the case is somewhat different, however, as the Ethiopian state is really a nineteenth century empire attempting to hold itself together. Powerful secessionist movements exist in at least three provinces, in addition to the revolutionary movement in Eritrea. The Marxist government is making little progress against, and may even be losing ground to, these movements.

The primary tension in the Zaire is between the inhabitants of Shaba province, which contains most of the country's mineral wealth, and the central government, which is dominated by other ethnic groups. Moreover, Shaba's natural economic links run not through the capital in the north, but rather to the south and west. The country is held together currently by President Mobutu and the army, which is the only national institution. The situation after Mobutu's death would be problematic.

The internal situation in Angola is very difficult. There is an existing civil war, based largely on ethnic divisions, which is having dire economic effects and for which it is very difficult to envisage a constructive solution. According to at least one of the experts, the territorial integrity of Angola is very uncertain.

Nigeria continues to struggle for unity in the face of historic conflicts between the Muslim northern tribes, which dominate the armed forces, and other tribes, which largely control the country's economic resources. One expert suggested that the coup in Nigeria in 1983 was another manifestation of this struggle and reflects the northern tribes' concern that if civilian rule continued, a nonnortherner would take office in 1987. There was, of course, a very

costly civil war in Nigeria in the late 1960s, and
no real power-sharing arrangement has ever been
implemented successfully. However, the war was so
costly in lives and suffering that there are great
disincentives against a renewal of fighting,
thereby making Nigeria the least likely of the
four problem states to suffer significant internal
violence.

The consequences of these internal problems
are hard to predict and would depend on the
circumstances that attended a crisis in any of
these nations. Chronic conflict and turmoil are
one possibility. The actual creation of smaller,
new states is a second, and the restructuring of
individual nations into some sort of confederation
would be a third. (In all cases, however, these
problems suggest opportunities for Soviet or Cuban
intervention.) One may go so far as to suggest
that the very concept of nation-states may be
slowly decomposing in Africa. There is, after
all, no a priori reason to expect this European
model to take root in African circumstances. If
national governments cannot deliver the services
that Africans have been taught to expect from
them, they may for all practical purposes lose all
vestiges of authority. The chronic turmoil and
lawlessness that have characterized nations like
Uganda for a long time, and Ghana more recently,
may presage a broader trend in many parts of the
continent.

Declining French influence in African
political/military affairs also is to be expected.
The French position in Africa in the 1980s is
similar to the British position in the Persian
Gulf in the 1960s--that is, nearing the end of its
decisive phase. France will continue to exert
economic and cultural influence in much of the
continent, but French resources are too limited to
permit France to maintain its past role as
defender of the political status quo. The French
government's unsuccessful attempt to maneuver the
United States into assuming France's traditional
responsibilities in Chad in the fall of 1983 was
perhaps the first demonstration of this decline.
In the future, either the United States will

become more directly involved in African affairs
or no Western power will play a significant role.

The most important uncertainty in African
relations is the prospective level of violence in
the southern part of the continent. Although
unlikely, a sudden and massive escalation of
violence within South Africa is possible and could
grow large enough to cause the exodus of a substantial portion of the white population, the
installation of a very brutal and repressive
successor white regime, and the extension of
military conflict to other nations in the region.
Such events could result from widespread, almost
spontaneous civil disorders within South Africa,
if they were combined with relatively successful
guerrilla attacks on urban targets. Although
families of Dutch ancestry (the majority of the
white population) have lived in South Africa for a
century or more and for the most part will not
leave the country voluntarily, a substantial
portion of the white population are relatively
recent immigrants from former Portuguese territories in Africa and Rhodesia (now Zimbabwe).
This white minority remains despite the threat of
violence because of the high living standards
enjoyed by the white population and because they
believe that if the violence were to reach a level
where it could not be contained, the European
governments would come to the aid of the South
African government. However, large-scale violence
within South Africa could transform both these
conditions and result in large-scale emigration--
particularly by the younger generation--and the
creation of a far more difficult situation.

The implications of such an eventuality for
U.S. military planning are twofold. Opportunities
for Soviet intervention in support of the
guerrilla movement and also in defense of the
bordering nations would be greatly expanded; and
there also would be direct and indirect threats to
the security of Western sources of strategic
minerals found predominantly in southern Africa,
including chromium, cobalt, gold, and platinum.

LATIN AMERICA

The experts drew a mixed picture of the future strategic environment in Latin America. The surprise-free forecast for Central America and the Caribbean is bleak, largely because of the region's overpopulation and crushing economic problems, as well as the support for revolutionary movements provided by Cuba and by other Communist regimes. As a result, there is likely to be continued political instability and internal conflict in several nations and--depending primarily upon the policies pursued by the United States--the possibility of one or two additional Marxist-Leninist regimes before the end of the century. U.S. relations with Cuba can be expected to remain tense. Further to the south, however, the outlook is more optimistic from the standpoint of U.S. interests. In the surprise-free scenario, renewed economic growth is possible, as is the further development of more stable, civilian controlled, democratic political systems in many nations of South America. In the near-term, however, fulfillment of this expectation depends upon the conclusion of a durable solution to the international debt situation. Future events in Brazil, which could have a major impact on both economic and political developments throughout the continent, remain uncertain.

Central America

The future course of events in Central America and the Caribbean is unlikely to support U.S. interests given the region's economic prospects; there are virtually no grounds for optimism in this regard and, considering the continuing population pressures in many of the nations of the region, substantial reasons for despair. As one expert stated: "Central American countries are desperately poor for the most part, and simply do not have the resources to take-off. Past models of economic success in the hemisphere, such as Venezuela, depended on a source of significant revenues--no such source is in prospect in Central America."

There are problems other than economic ones as well, particularly Cuba's support for the region's revolutionary movements. Domestically, notwithstanding recent successful elections in El Salvador and Guatemala, small elites are expected to continue dominating these countries and to refuse the sort of democratically-oriented domestic policies necessary to build stable political systems. As a result, continued instability and domestic violence and the emergence of one or two additional Marxist-Leninist regimes are the most likely scenarios for the remainder of this century. El Salvador, Guatemala, and Honduras (in addition to Nicaragua)--in that order--are the nations most likely to experience such a change. Panama and some of the Caribbean islands--notably Haiti--also might experience serious difficulties during the forecast period. In the surprise-free case, a wholesale regional shift to Cuban dominance is not expected. There are two reasons for this. First, it seems likely that the United States would react decisively in the event of the establishment of an additional Marxist-Leninist regime. Second, the Soviet Union is not in a position to underwrite the economies and military security of additional nations in the region.

Interestingly, in the surprise-free case there is little reason to expect that substantial violence or significant instability will spread to Mexico. The Mexican government has demonstrated its resiliency and stability during the recent financial crisis, and the ruling political party seems to have coopted much of the left's potential base of support, particularly the labor unions (the more violent leftist elements were suppressed during the 1970s). The Mexican formula for stability rests on a certain amount of revolutionary rhetoric and calculated demonstrations of independence from the United States (as evidenced by the tendency among Mexican presidents to differ publicly with their U.S. counterparts). But it also depends on a less visible, very practical approach to economic decisionmaking in which the needs of the different economic sectors are satisfied. According to one expert "The Mexican political system has gone through substantial change; there is no great oscillation between right and left. The state is now seen as the primary legitimizing institution, resting on the military, the PRI, and state-run economic enterprises." If anything, the further success of revolutionary movements in Central America would drive the Mexican government's policy farther to the right and generate new support for conservative elements.

Relations between the United States and Cuba can be expected to remain poor. No serious rapprochement between the two states appears possible so long as Fidel Castro remains in power, and there is no reason to expect Castro to do otherwise as long as his health is good. There is no evidence of popular alienation; the economic situation is bad, but not collapsing and not likely to become bad enough (because of Soviet support) to cause fundamental change. Castro appears absolutely committed to his role as a leader of world revolution and is not likely to compromise that position in the interest of better relations with the United States, no matter how enticing such a prospect might appear on economic grounds. Indeed, the Cuban leader appears to value U.S. hostility as a means of demonstrating his revolutionary elan and relevance. By now, moreover, Cuba is so firmly dependent on Soviet military and economic support that any future agreements with the United States that might required explicit limits on the Soviet military role in Cuba would be difficult to conclude. In addition, one of Fidel Castro's firmest demands is that Cuba be treated as the equal of the United States. From his perspective, this precludes any discussion of Cuba's relations with third nations or involvement in foreign situations. The only proper topics for U.S.-Cuban negotiations, he believes, are aspects of the bilateral relationship.

Any direct Soviet role in Central America in the surprise-free forecast is likely to be limited. The USSR will continue to support Cuba and, through Cuba, other Marxist regimes and revolutionary movements. The Soviet Union appears unwilling to accept major new economic responsibilities, however, and has made clear-- according to one expert--its unwillingness to risk a military confrontation with the United States to defend Nicaragua or any additional Marxist-Leninist government in the region.

This outlook for Central America and the Caribbean, like all the forecasts, is far from certain. On the one hand, the United States may become unwilling or unable to act in support of existing governments in the region, in which case revolutionary forces could make major breakthroughs. Under such circumstances, Marxist-Leninist governments might be established in El Salvador, Guatemala, Haiti, Honduras, Panama, and perhaps other Caribbean island-nations. This extensive a revolutionary breakthrough could threaten Mexico's stability and in this "worst case" lead to widespread violence in Mexico. It also is conceivable--although extremely unlikely, even in such a scenario--that the USSR would be sufficiently emboldened by the U.S. inaction to establish a more threatening military presence in the region. The implications for U.S. military planning obviously would be severe.

Alternatively, in a more promising scenario, an activist U.S. policy could lead to the containment of revolutionary movements, progress toward social reform in the nations of the region, and the gradual achievement of greater stability and economic growth. In this case, Nicaragua probably would remain under its present government but pursue more moderate policies, internally and externally, and evolve along the model of Algeria--a nation fiercely revolutionary in rhetoric, but equally pragmatic in its relations with other countries. Cuba would not necessarily change in this scenario, although its influence would be contained. Eventually, it also might assume a more pragmatic stance in world affairs.

South America

The surprise-free outlook farther south in the hemisphere is more promising than in Central America, although still far from certain. The emergence of seemingly stable, democratic political systems in several countries--Colombia, Ecuador, and Venezuela--seems to portend a favorable future. Other nations also are witnessing movement toward civilian-controlled, democratic rule; the accession of a popularly elected civilian government in Argentina in 1984 and Brazil's continued transition toward full democracy are cited in support of this thesis. (Chile is a notable exception to this trend.) In some cases, the trend toward democratization has resulted from the past failures of military regimes, particularly in the economic sphere, although the failures of the Argentine armed forces were more far-ranging. The future seems to promise, in this view, the rise in several countries of mass political parties incorporating pluralistic elements. Previously, Latin American political parties tended to reflect the personal following of a single individual, a type of political organization that does not ensure long-term political stability.

Resumed economic progress is likely in South America in the near term, at least for most countries. Peru is a notable exception to this forecast and is the least stable of the countries of the continent. Countries heavily dependent for export earnings on single commodities whose markets are depressed--Bolivia's tin, Chile's copper, and Venezuela's oil--also may recover only slowly. Indeed, as noted in Chapter 2, technological trends may ensure continued constraints on economic growth in these countries. Much depends on the degree to which the U.S. recovery is sustained (thus assuring better markets for South American goods) and also on whether or not a durable solution to the international debt crisis is devised and implemented successfully.

The resumption of economic progress and democratic rule in South America does not suggest the return of the former U.S. dominance of these country's foreign policies. Indeed, the nations of South America are likely to pursue increasingly independent policies involving closer ties with European countries, and Japan for some nations, and a leadership role of greater prominence in the Third World for others. Brazil could become especially important in the latter context, at least in the surprise-free forecast. Active Brazilian ties with some nations in the Middle East (notably Iraq) and Africa (notably Angola and Mozambique) at present are likely forerunners of future trends.

Both the Cuban and Soviet roles in South America are likely to be circumscribed. Cuba maintains relations with some nations and supports some revolutionary movements--M-19 in Colombia is the most prominent--but the situation in the South is very different than that in Central America. The Soviet Union's role is likely to remain largely commercial. Trade between the USSR and several South American countries has been expanding in recent years and is expected to continue growing. This trend is not expected to confer political influence, however, and often takes place with the most vehemently outspoken anticommunist governments (e.g., the former military regime of Argentina). Opportunities for Soviet military involvement in South America in the surprise-free forecast are limited. The one substantial Soviet arms transaction in the past-- to Peru in the mid-1970s--is generally viewed as evidence of the inappropriateness of Soviet equipment. To the extent that South American countries wish to move away from dependence on U.S. equipment, they will turn primarily to sources in Western Europe for technologically advanced weapons and to local producers-- especially Brazil and Argentina--for standard equipment.

The relatively optimistic picture described for South America is far from certain. As noted, much depends on a successful resolution of the debt problem and on a sustained U.S. economic recovery. A failure in either could result in a serious economic situation and the political instabilities that would be associated with it. Technological advances also may inflict structural constraints on Latin American economies. The increasing application of ceramics and manmade materials may impose permanent restrictions on the potential export earnings of those Latin American countries that depend on mineral experts (Chile, Bolivia) and, thus, on the capital available for their economic development.

Brazil's uncertain future is a key to future developments in the region. Although relatively well off because of its huge resources (other than energy, which is a serious problem), Brazil may never fulfill its population's expectation of becoming a world power. The Brazilian elite represents a sophisticated and dynamic culture, but there are also huge masses of very poor people in Brazil whose circumstances and resulting political disquiet greatly restrict Brazil's ability to play a leading external role. The process of transition to civilian rule is still far from assured, and the possibilities of either a return to strict military rule or the outbreak of significant internal violence cannot be ignored. Brazil is preparing nonetheless to play a larger role in South American affairs, partic-ularly with those countries bordering the Amazon basin. In fact, Brazil could become a major actor on the global scene in the twenty-first century. Whether or not this actually transpires may well depend on events during the next ten years.

Economic failure in South America, if pro-longed, could lead to internal, politically motivated violence in several countries, notably Brazil, and a greater danger of international conflict as well. There are several existing, if quiescent, disputes within the region, any of which could heat up suddenly. In this context, the conclusion drawn by both the Nuclear Proliferation Panel convened for this study and the Latin

American experts interviewed—that both Argentina and Brazil are likely to develop nuclear weapons before the end of the century—could prove ominous.

4

Alternative Composite Futures

The strategic environment for U.S. military planning in the next century will be shaped largely by the key variables identified in the preceding chapters: (1) technological advances in the United States, in other industrialized nations, and in the USSR; (2) the relative rate and composition of economic growth in the industrial nations and the amount of resources that each is willing to allocate for defense; (3) trends in the dependencies of the United States and its allies on foreign sources of critical commodities; (4) the proliferation of nuclear and advanced conventional military capabilities; (5) public attitudes in this country toward foreign policy and commitments abroad; and (6) economic, demographic, and societal trends worldwide. No doubt there are many other factors that will affect the international environment twenty years from now, but these six appear to be particularly important.

The possible conditions implied by these factors can give rise to a large number of alternative composite futures. Not all can be fully developed in any single document, and there is no obvious rule to guide selection of the most interesting permutations. Insofar as the primary purpose of this study is to examine the implications of alternative futures for U.S. military planning, we have selected alternatives for detailed development that have wide-ranging effects on the desirability of different types of

force structures. Taken together, the five
alternatives described in this chapter provide a
reasonable means of testing the adequacy of
current and proposed military plans in
environments that would most greatly stress
alternative force structures and military
strategies.

These five alternative strategic environments
have been constructed by combining possible
relationships in the six regions of the world with
alternative assumptions about U.S. involvement in
world affairs. Developments in each region are
characterized either as the surprise-free forecast
described in Chapter 3 or as one of the key
potential variations also discussed there. The
experts interviewed for this study generally
agreed that U.S. policy was the most important
single determinant of the course of world events,
which accounts for the elevation of the "activist
isolationist" factor as one of the major variables
in the construction of alternative scenarios.
Aside from this broad characterization of U.S.
policy (activist/isolationist), capabilities and
constraints on U.S. policy are not used as
structural determinants of alternative futures but
rather are discussed within each postulated
environment as possible sources of variations. In
some cases, there is a logical connection between
the hypothesized strategic environment and a
specific end state of a U.S. capability or
constraint. In others, a U.S. capability or
constraint can range widely and not influence the
basic structural character of the hypothesized
strategic environment.

The basic characteristics of the five
alternative strategic environments are summarized
in Table 4.1 and discussed in the following five
sections of this chapter. Each section includes a
preliminary description of the implications of the
alternative environment for U.S. military
planning. These judgments are tentative and
exemplary. A precise determination of which
specific force posture would be most effective in
a particular strategic environment must be based
upon far more detailed and rigorous analyses than

Table 4.1. ALTERNATIVE STRATEGIC ENVIRONMENTS

Variable / Case	U.S. Policy	Europe	USSR	East and South Asia	Middle East	Africa	Latin America
Extrapolation	Activist	Surprise-Free	Surprise-Free	Surprise-Free	Surprise-Free	Surprise-Free	Surprise-Free
Third World in Disarray	Activist	Surprise-Free	Surprise-Free	• Disintegration on Rim	• Fundamentalist Resurgence	• Upheaval in South	• Breakdown in South
USSR Resurgent	Activist	• Germany Neutralized	• Break-Out	• China Destabilized	• Arab-Israeli Regession	• Upheaval in South	• Cuban Breakthrough
Anarchic	Isolationist	• West European Defense Entity; • Violence in East	• Domestic Disorder	• China Destabilized; • Japan Assertive • Distegration on Rim	• Fundamentalist Resurgence; • Arab-Israeli Regession	• Upheaval in South	• Breakdown in South; • Cuban Breakthrough
Optimistic	Activist	• Violence in East	Surprise-Free	Surprise-Free +	Surprise-Free	Surprise-Free	• Rollback in Central America

Additional constraints and opportunities: Technology, resource dependencies, U.S. economic performance, defense spending, nuclear proliferation.

were feasible in this study. The study concludes with the author's personal views of the likely character of political/military relations at the end of the century.

ALTERNATIVE ONE: AN EXTRAPOLATION FROM PRESENT TRENDS

Current trends in the various regions of the world suggest a relatively benign environment for U.S. security interests at the turn of the century. This is not to say that there will not be considerable strife in world affairs, serious military threats posed to U.S. national security, and many situations in which important U.S. interests are jeopardized. The world of the surprise-free forecasts remains a violent and dangerous place, a world in which military power continues to play an absolutely vital role in protecting the nation and its interests abroad. The surprise-free forecasts do suggest, however, that the United States and its allies have considerable influence in world affairs. This influence derives from the country's tremendous economic leverage (particularly that provided by the private sector), from the nation's techno-logical prowess and organizational competence, and from the many attractive political and cultural manifestations of a dynamic society. All these elements of U.S. national power contribute to the international environment so that U.S. military power can remain most often in the background of international events; this power is a determinant of international status and position to be sure, but one whose greatest effectiveness is marked by the absence of explicit tests of its sufficiency.

The relative optimism of the surprise-free forecasts also results from the expected weakness of the Soviet Union. As one Soviet expert remarked, "The Russian century is over. They face increasing problems. Their prospects are dim for the rest of the century. This does not mean they are not dangerous, but strategically there is little going for them." Soviet weaknesses are manifold. Many in Eastern Europe, and perhaps

some groups in parts of the USSR, refuse to
discard their nationalistic aspirations in favor
of a professed ideological bond, even in the face
of decades of Soviet repression and seemingly
omnipotent Soviet military power. The Soviet
economic system is falling farther and farther
behind those in all other parts of the industrial
world. According to some sources, the average
standard of living is declining in the USSR.
There are reports of food shortages and widespread
outbreaks of disease. Birthrates have declined
precipitously, infant mortality is rising, and
life expectancy is on the decline. Most importantly, Soviet weakness stems from a political
system so stultified it cannot adapt to contemporary circumstances or make changes to avoid
further setbacks. The result is a continuing
decline in Soviet economic prospects and growing
tension between the Soviet regime and the Russian
people. The latter are becoming increasingly
aware of the differences between their lives and
the lives of people in so many other parts of the
world--as well as of the great disparities between
the Soviet elite and the great mass of Soviet
citizens. Internationally, the weaknesses of the
Soviet system in the surprise-free forecast lead
to dwindling opportunities abroad, as even
officials of left-wing political parties become
increasingly suspicious of Soviet motives and
skeptical of the putative benefits of alliance
with the Soviet state. In the words of one Soviet
expert, "The Russian system cannot take hold
anywhere, except in the form of direct puppets
supported by Soviet military power. Even Angola
and Ethiopia--tailor made for them--are not
becoming permanent advances for the USSR."

These serious problems notwithstanding, the
USSR can be expected to remain powerful militarily, a force to be reckoned with in many
potential situations. Although the Soviet Union
may become more inwardly directed--a result of its
substantial domestic problems and a more realistic
attitude among the leadership regarding the
state's ability to sustain positions in various
parts of the world--the USSR will continue to
participate actively in world affairs and to cling

tenaciously to several positions that Soviet
leaders deem essential to their national security
and international position. Continued dominance
of Eastern Europe is the most vital of these
interests, and Soviet footholds in the Western
Hemisphere (Cuba) and in East Asia (Vietnam) are
probably critical as well. Nor will Soviet
leaders give up their long term objectives of
decoupling the United States from its allies in
Europe and Asia and crippling this nation's
ability to organize and lead the opposition to
Soviet world dominance. Soviet leaders also will
insist on being treated appropriately, by which
they mean as the equal of the United States. The
new generation of Soviet leaders now taking the
reins of power is unlikely to share past
generations' adversity to risk, at least to the
same degree, and may be more confident of Soviet
military power and of the leadership's right to
exercise that power in support of Soviet
interests--a formula, under certain circumstances,
that could lead to confrontations.

Soviet failures do not necessarily translate
into U.S. successes. The world is not anything
like a zero-sum game of two players, and even in
this extrapolated scenario there would be many
sources of competition and conflict for the United
States independent of Soviet machinations. Events
in the Third World can inflict penalties on either
or both of the great powers, and even among
industrial nations, the expectation is that most
countries will exercise greater autonomy, their
continued reliance on U.S. or Soviet security
guarantees notwithstanding.

A key component of these surprise-free
forecasts is the assumption that the basic global
structure of alliances will remain unchanged, that
the fundamental relationships among the United
States, the nations of Europe, the USSR, and Japan
will evolve, but not really be altered in any
basic way. There will be strains within NATO as
the alliance searches for a satisfactory solution
to its defense problems within the constraints
imposed by relatively tight financial limits, an
active and powerful antinuclear movement, and the

genuine economic and political differences that always arise among democratic and necessarily competitive nations. These problems, however, are not expected to become so severe as to disrupt the crucial perception on the part of both the United States and the nations of Western Europe that the benefits of membership and active participation in NATO far exceed its sometimes exasperating political frictions and perceived costs and liabilities. This judgment may be accounted for by the forecast that it will prove possible to adjust current military postures and the distribution of defense burdens within NATO without precipitating a political crisis.

The U.S. alliance with Japan may undergo even greater strains, especially in terms of economic and technological competition, but with the same result--a continued alliance and close coordination of the two nations' diplomatic, political, and military policies. Japan is expected to remain only weakly armed, if economically powerful, and to continue relying on the United States for its security. The United States will maintain that guarantee and the forces necessary to make it credible, despite recurrent economic problems with Japan and popular perceptions in this nation that we are shouldering an unfair burden.

Soviet relations with the industrial world are expected to remain strained and relations with Japan to remain cold. A settlement of the dispute about the Northern Territories is virtually unimaginable; without it, there can be no real rapprochement between the two states. According to this view, Soviet relations with China will remain formally correct, but distant, thereby requiring the continued allocation of substantial resources to Soviet defenses in Asia.

East European nationalism will continue to be a potent force, periodically threatening, in its many expressions, to reach a point at which the Soviets decide to intervene overtly to suppress an East European protest movement. Because of their weaknesses at home and abroad, Soviet leaders can be expected to avoid such violent incidents, however, thus causing them to tolerate a greater degree of economic and political diversity among their Warsaw Pact allies than they might in different circumstances. Assuming that an overt Soviet intervention in Eastern Europe does not occur, relations between East and West, if not between the United States and USSR, are likely to deepen and widen. Trade as well as humanitarian contacts of various sorts--some between private institutions such as churches and professional associations--will flourish. Better relations will not diminish the fundamental antipathy between the two sides, however, and therefore the determination of both East and West to maintain their respective military preparedness will persevere as well. Increasingly close ties between the two German states will serve as the leading edge of this gradual expansion of cooperation between East and West, although the renewed recognition of a common German identity is not likely to go so far as to make possible the creation of a unified German state. If these assessments prove accurate, the risk of conflict between East and West in Europe should remain relatively low; a Soviet intervention to suppress an uprising in Eastern Europe is the most serious potential contingency.

The most significant uncertainty in the Third World concerns future Chinese policies. In this surprise-free future, China will maintain its current pragmatic policies, both domestically and internationally. Continuing reforms of the Chinese economic and political system will make possible an economic growth rate sufficient to outstrip population increases and gradually improve both China's industrial position and the quality of life experienced by the majority of its people. China's armed forces also will be gradually modernized in the surprise-free scenario, although not at a rate that would threaten either the USSR or China's other neighbors in Asia--especially Japan.

A similarly optimistic forecast obtains for most other nations in Asia. Rapid economic growth

and gradually increasing political stability will
characterize the nations of South and East Asia.
Nations presently threatened by internal strife,
such as India, the Philippines, and Indonesia, are
likely in this composite future to elude political
turmoil and domestic violence on a nation-
threatening scale. (This benign forecast,
however, should be considered in light of the view
that both India and Pakistan are likely to acquire
nuclear weapons before the end of the century.)

The Middle East, in a surprise-free future,
would witness the gradual emergence of pragmatic
and secular policies, the strengthening of
moderate regimes and their increasingly close
cooperation, and the dampening of existing
conflicts--both those between Arabs and Israelis
and between religious fundamentalists and
individuals with more modernist perspectives.
This forecast is particularly promising given the
projections presented in Chapter 2 and suggests
that both Japan and most nations in Western Europe
will remain substantially dependent upon Middle
Eastern sources of petroleum throughout the
century. Although it may take one more military
conflict between Israel and Syria to make the
outcome feasible, a de facto peace between Arabs
and Israelis is the most likely prospect in the
surprise-free future. As such, terrorism,
especially its more dangerous and recent form--
terrorism sponsored by nation-states--will
diminish. Broad projections like these, however,
cannot account for idiosyncratic courses of action
followed by individual nations.

The surprise-free forecasts for other regions
of the Third World are less optimistic. Prospects
are most bleak in Africa and Central America. In
both regions, there appears to be little hope of
substantial progress toward the alleviation of
extremely serious population pressures and
economic shortcomings. Thus, great societal
unrest, chronic domestic insurgencies and other
forms of domestic violence, and the extension of
Soviet influence through the provision of military
and diplomatic support will be the case.
Nevertheless, the Soviet position in Africa is not

likely to improve measurably in the surprise-free scenario, largely because both regional leaders and Soviet officials recognize the USSR's limited ability to help these countries ease their desperate economic situations.

The presence of a communist Cuba and Fidel Castro's willingness to sacrifice Cuban national interests in the cause of "world revolution" make the outlook in Central America more disturbing. This surprise-free scenario is likely to witness the establishment of one or two additional Marxist-Leninist regimes in Central America, but neither insurgency, major domestic violence, nor serious political instabilities are likely to spread to Mexico.

In the remainder of Latin America, prospects are more promising. There is a clear trend toward greater democratization and political stability and, assuming that the current international debt problem is resolved successfully, recovery and sustained economic growth can resume in South America, making possible both domestic tranquility and the amelioration of international conflicts in the region. The course of economic and political events in Brazil will be key in determining the accuracy of this forecast. Moreover, the South American forecast does not really address the consequences of nuclear proliferation in the region. Assuming that both Argentina and Brazil will probably acquire nuclear weapon capabilities before the end of the century, the implications for stability in South America might be troubling

All in all, the experts projected only limited opportunities for the Soviet Union in the surprise-free strategic environment and only limited ability within the USSR to take advantage of those opportunities that do arise. The surprise-free scenario is one in which relative economic capabilities are the dominant force in world affairs. Relative military power--to say nothing of such intangible factors as religious movements--although important, takes a distinct second place to the basic realities of the distribution of the world's resources and the knowledge of how best to organize society to exploit available resources. From such a perspective, the United States is in a greatly advantaged position vis-a-vis the Soviet Union. The next century may witness the gradual transformation of world politics from the basic structure established by the U.S.-Soviet competition to a system organized more fundamentally around competing economic groups. The leading edge of this competition is likely to involve the United States (with the possibly support of the West European nations) on the one hand, in opposition to a grouping of East Asian nations (not including China) under the leadership of Japan on the other. In such a system, the Soviet bloc of nations would be a less important third party--always capable of disrupting events because of its military power and therefore dangerous, but not really a central player in the normal course of events.

The transition from the present system to such a radically different one, however, and indeed the basic fulfillment of the surprise-free scenario through the end of this century, is based on several assumptions, the most crucial of which is that the United States will continue to play an active role in world politics and that the elements in U.S. public opinion that favor isolationist policies will be contained. Second, the United States will continue to allocate substantial expenditures to defense, expenditures that to some segments of the U.S. public may appear excessive, particularly when compared to allied defense spending. Finally, it is assumed that the improvements in U.S. military capabilities forecast by the Delphi technology panel will in fact be accomplished and that the United States will maintain its technological edge over the Soviet Union. If these surprise-free technological forecasts were not fulfilled, the prospects for maintaining an acceptable military balance would diminish substantially and so, too, would the prospects for maintaining the favorable political/military relationships envisioned in this composite future.

Implications for U.S. Military Planning

In this composite surprise-free environment, the relative balance of military power, for the most part, would remain a backdrop for diplomatic activity. Generally speaking, the assumptions currently governing decisions on U.S. military forces would be upheld, and thus the present basis for force planning would be fulfilled. The U.S. posture could continue to develop along the general lines now envisioned. In the absence of dramatic events to make clear the need and benefits of military preparedness, however, relatively tight limits are likely to continue to constrain the amount of resources made available to defense in the United States, meaning that hard choices would have to be made among competing military requirements and strategies.

The search for a stable strategic nuclear deterrent at reduced but modernized force levels should continue to receive emphasis, both through arms programs and negotiations. No events foreseen in the surprise-free strategic environment would cause the United States to depart from its present emphasis on a balanced triad of offensive central nuclear forces and the maintenance of theater nuclear capabilities comparable to those of the adversary. Although research should continue on the advanced technologies that might contribute to the establishment of effective ballistic missile defenses, the technological forecast and the necessity to choose among competing defense requirements suggest that the actual deployment of a major missile defense system should be deferred until well into the next century.

In Europe, an adjustment of military contributions, tactics, and force postures would be possible, although no radical change should be expected—the alliance would have little reason to depart substantially from its basic strategy of "flexible response." Steps to make full use of emerging conventional weapon, sensor, and command and control technologies to raise the nuclear

threshold in Europe should be pursued vigorously.
Some U.S. forces could be returned to the United
States as a result of adjustments in NATO plans
and force postures without causing undue political
disruption within the alliance. Some of these
forces could be equipped and trained to respond
rapidly in the event of a crisis in Europe; others
could be designated for use in crises in other
theaters as well. Basically, the United States
could rely increasingly on forces based in the
United States in a high state of readiness to
respond to crises worldwide. Fiscal constraints
on defense resources alone should cause the United
States to move in this direction. The requirement
that forces be used flexibly around the world also
would stress the allocation of resources for
airlift, fast sealift, and--especially for
European contingencies--sea control forces.

The United States also should continue to
maintain a forward defense posture in Asia and to
cooperate with treaty allies and other friendly
governments. The alliance with Japan should
remain the bedrock of the U.S. position in Asia,
with substantial and continuing U.S. force
deployments both in Japan and Korea. The relative
stability expected in East Asia also would permit
retention of the major U.S. bases in the
Philippines. Although some improvements could be
expected in the Japanese force posture, the
current modest size and defensive orientation of
Japan's armed forces are not likely to change
during the forecast period.

Only relatively small forces would have to be
maintained exclusively for contingencies in the
Third World, as major upheavals would not be
expected. Present policies to improve the flexibility with which forces could be employed and to
create an array of forces appropriate for the full
range of contingencies would be continued.
Security assistance to friends and allies in the
Third World probably would be increased, thereby
requiring increases in U.S. training missions and
joint military exercises around the globe.
Terrorism would remain a serious problem, and the
United States consequently would have to improve

its means of dealing with this form of interstate
violence. Both cooperative international agreements and better unilateral military capabilities
tailored to these contingencies would be
mandatory.

ALTERNATIVE TWO: DISORDER IN THE THIRD WORLD

    In this composite future, relations among the
major industrial nations will proceed as described
in the surprise-free environment. The Soviet
Union tends toward weakness and internal
preoccupation but remains hostile toward the
United States, Western Europe, and Japan;
nationalism remains strong in Eastern Europe; ties
between East and West in Europe, and particularly
in Germany, deepen; and despite strains of one
sort or another, the basic Western alliance
structure remains sound. It is further
hypothesized, however, that events in parts of the
Third World do not proceed in the relatively
optimistic fashion projected in the surprise-free
forecasts. Rapid population growth in several
regions creates social pressures resulting in mass
migrations both within nations and across national
boundaries. Faltering rates of economic
development and a widening gap between the rich
and the poor give rise to popular disquiet,
political upheaval, and a fertile field for
demagogues. Social movements espousing revolutionary ideologies, some advocating terrorism and
other forms of mass violence, gain a greater
audience. What exactly might go wrong in these
regions is hard to predict, but a number of the
more disturbing possibilities were suggested in
the individual discussions of each region.

    Most threatening would be possible events in
the Middle East. As discussed in Chapter 3, there
is a fine balance in several nations of the Middle
East at present between forces pressing for
moderate, pragmatic policies that promise gradual
economic development and slow improvements in the
everyday lives of the masses of people and those
more radical elements that propose instant

salvation through nationalism, ideology, or religion. Fundamentalist Islam has become increasingly popular in many countries, and it is certainly possible that during the next twenty years the world may witness successful fundamentalist revolutions in several nations-- Egypt, Pakistan, the Sudan, and Tunisia are considered by many experts to be the most likely candidates. The possibility of a successful revolution in Saudi Arabia and other Persian Gulf states may be somewhat lower, but would be even more costly in terms of U.S. interests.

The radicalization of Egypt or Saudi Arabia, or of several of the less important states, could alter the prospect for political/military relations in the region greatly. It would mean that the present Iranian regime would almost certainly survive the death of its founder, the Ayatollah Khomeini--a less certain possibility otherwise. Radicalization would lead to a substantial increase in state-sponsored terrorism throughout the region and beyond, as well as a grave escalation of the Arab-Israeli conflict. There would probably not be an increase in opportunities for Soviet expansionism, as shown by the cool relations between Iran and the USSR at present.

But the main dangers of such a trend are unpredictable. Governments motivated primarily by extraworldly or ideal objectives are capable of quite astounding actions, as illustrated during the early 1980s by the Iran-Iraq war. Many such actions could threaten U.S. interests. If Saudi Arabia were among the nations that succumbed to a fundamentalist revolution, oil exports would be used more pointedly as a weapon of statecraft, a development that could threaten the security of Japan and some West European countries directly, impose grave economic costs on the entire industrialized world and many Third World nations, and conceivably make the pursuit of some U.S. policies, such as the support of Israel, more difficult.

Other dangers also might be associated with a renewal of the fundamentalist tide. Although the extent and direction of these threats to U.S. citizens and their interests in the region are hard to predict, it is important to recall that Pakistan, one of the nations most likely to have acquired a nuclear capability by the end of the century, also is considered a primary candidate for a fundamentalist regime. Pakistan's acquisition of nuclear weapons, particularly if the nation were then governed by a crusading Islamic government, could have implications for the level of support provided to insurgents in Soviet-occupied Afghanistan and, for that matter, for stability in South Asia generally. The latter, in fact, could be the scene of considerable trouble in this alternative composite future. In addition to the postulated change in the Pakistani government, the scenario envisions considerable instability in India and a possibility that the nation actually would devolve into several independent states. Pakistan under a fundamentalist government could be expected to try strengthening nearly any forces within India that sought greater autonomy. Depending on the precise status and distribution of India's own nuclear weapon program, (it is assumed by virtually all our experts that India will have produced a substantial nuclear stockpile before the end of the century), the situation could become extremely dangerous. Other nations in East Asia are also assumed to have been destabilized in this alternative strategic environment. Indonesia and the Philippines would be the most likely candidates for internal violence and turmoil.

Other trouble spots that might witness serious interstate conflict in this scenario include southern Africa, where a significant escalation of the racial conflict is eminently feasible. This almost certainly would lead to economic disarray, disruptions in the production of strategic minerals, and opportunities for Soviet intervention. Finally, one might postulate in this scenario a reversal of currently favorable trends in South America, a reversal that would lead to economic stagnation, political turmoil in

several countries, notably Brazil, and the
possible initiation of conflicts among several
pairs of nations in the region.

The consequences of all this for U.S.
interests could be severe. Most grave might be
the potential for nuclear proliferation and, in
fact, for the possible initiation of a nuclear
war. If the most dangerous expression of this
scenario became a reality, the actual use of
nuclear weapons in South Asia would be a distinct
possibility, as it also would be in the Middle
East. Even nuclear detonations in Latin America
and southern Africa would be possibilities.
Although the United States certainly could avoid
any direct involvement in such conflicts, breaches
of the present forty-year sanction against the use
of nuclear weapons have worrisome implications for
longterm security interests. The United States
also could be harmed by setbacks in its worldwide
military position. The loss of key bases in the
Philippines would be a distinct possibility. So,
too, would be the loss of access and overflight
rights as well as other military arrangements with
several key countries in southwest Asia and
northern Africa.

There are also economic risks to U.S.
interests posed in this scenario. Supplies of
petroleum and sources of certain critical minerals
would be jeopardized in this alternative future.
Interruptions in the normal resource production
and distribution system would be threatened simply
by instability and probable violence in southern
Africa and the Persian Gulf region. The
likelihood that nations might attempt to
manipulate supplies deliberately for policy
objectives would be much greater. Either way,
unless alternative sources or stockpiles had been
prepared, the economic consequences of such
actions could be severe.

Finally, even broader threats to U.S.
interests in the next century would be raised by
this scenario, for the international relationships
that it postulates by the year 2000 are unlikely
to be very stable. Given the turmoil on its

southern borders, for example, and signs of trouble in East Asia, China might consider alternative security arrangements--rapprochement with the Soviet Union would be one possibility. Japan, too, might reconsider its close alliance with the United States if the former nation proved unable to contend with the rising level of violence and turmoil that would characterize much of the Third World, particularly Japan's petroleum sources in southwest Asia.

For all these reasons, if this scenario ever unfolded, the United States would attempt to intervene in at least some of these situations early on (remember, we are postulating an activist U.S. foreign policy) to protect its national and economic interests, to defend embattled friendly regimes, to disrupt facilities and production systems that were being established to produce nuclear weapons, and to shore-up its political position and alliance system. In most cases, given our assumption concerning the continued weaknesses and internal preoccupations of the Soviet Union, active Soviet military opposition would not be anticipated. Rather, in this future environment, emphasis on U.S. military planning should be placed on relatively light forces that could be moved quickly to and operate flexibly in a variety of potential trouble spots. In view of the prospective limitations on U.S. military facilities in these unstable regions, mobility forces, naval forces, and long-range strike aircraft also would be valued highly.

Implications for U.S. Military Planning

Given that there would be a greater likelihood in this composite future that nuclear capabilities might be found in the hands of extremely hostile, and possibly irrational, governments, it would be desirable to see greater emphasis in the United States on the development of missile and aircraft defense systems. Research and development of advanced technologies for these purposes should be accelerated, and, if the results were promising, the deployment of a major system could begin before the end of the century.

With the Third World in diarray, but conditions in Europe relatively stable and cooperative, primary attention in U.S. military planning should shift from the current NATO focus. South and East Asia and the Middle East would demand primary attention; southern Africa also would require greater U.S. military capabilities. West Europeans and the Japanese would share U.S. concerns about growing instabilities in Third World regions, particularly in view of their dependence on these regions for critical resources. European governments and peoples presumably would be willing to assist in attempts to reduce turbulence and encourage greater stability. Initially, they would no doubt prefer that their role outside Europe be a nonmilitary one that emphasizes economic and technical policies. As such, they might be expected to pick up more of the defense burden in Europe, thus facilitating a stronger U.S. military response worldwide. However, in time, European-U.S. military cooperation outside the current NATO geographic guidelines might increase as well. Security assistance could be one avenue for such cooperation, and coordinated naval deployments could be a second.

In East Asia, the United States could increase pressures on Japan to share a larger portion of the defense burden and to strengthen the joint military effectiveness of the two nations. The Japanese could be asked to take on additional defensive maritime roles along with an expanded role in missions more directly related to the defense of Japan, such as air defense. Strengthened U.S. naval forces in the Pacific and Indian Ocean would be desirable in this strategic environment. Given the relative stability that would characterize European affairs and the presumed greater contributions of the European members of NATO, some of this increase might be implemented by drawing down forces in the Atlantic. Moreover, in view of the potential loss of such currently friendly governments in East

Asia as the Philippines, the United States may have to direct substantial efforts in its foreign relations to securing access to new facilities in order to support sustained operations in South and East Asian waters. Bases in Australia might be one possibility.

The United States also could be expected to place greater emphasis on programs intended to strengthen the military capabilities of those governments in the Third World that remained friendly. U.S.-Korean cooperation, for example, could be stepped up. Generally, security assistance programs would expand while joint and combined military exercises could be used extensively to demonstrate both the commitment and strength of the United States and its remaining allies. To be prepared for potential contingencies in Third World regions, the United States would require additional military forces equipped, trained, and ready to move rapidly to distant parts of the globe. Reliance on military forces based in the United States thus would increase, a condition dictated by the need for flexibility and responsiveness. Greater European concerns about worldwide threats to resources and political stability might make possible the withdrawal of additional U.S. troops from the Continent as compared to the surprise-free future, thus making possible the fulfillment of this requirement within or near currently contemplated resource constraints. For the most part, given the expectation in this environment that the Soviets would be reluctant to become involved in major conflicts in distant regions because of their own domestic problems, incremental U.S. forces for Third World contingencies could be relatively light, mobile, and readily sustainable. The U.S. Marine Corps and other ready strike forces would be called upon frequently. Both airlift and fast sealift would have to receive a high priority, as would forces to protect lift assets en route and to operate with them if committed to action.

Terrorism would be a significant danger in this alternative environment, and substantial improvements both in international arrangements to combat such violence and in U.S. military capabilities to deal with it would be necessary. Incentives to deal with terrorism at its source, particularly if terrorist elements appeared to be gaining access to nuclear capabilities (a very real danger in this environment), could be substantial. The U.S. military establishment would have to be prepared to implement any such policy decisively and effectively.

ALTERNATIVE THREE: THE USSR RESURGENT

The possibility that the USSR might break out of the systemic limitations that are the cause of the relatively passive role envisioned for it in the previous two strategic environments should certainly not be ruled out. Much could happen within the Soviet Union during the twenty-year period of this forecast. The current shift of power to a new generation of Soviet leaders and the consolidation of authority by Mikhail Gorbachev presage the possibility of a successful implementation of reforms necessary to rejuvenate the Soviet economy and political system. With luck, such changes could lead to the eventual integration of modern technologies throughout the Soviet civilian sector, a substantial expansion in agricultural output, relatively rapid and sustained economic growth, and a new, outward-looking, positive mood among the Russian people-- to say nothing of a more confident and aggressive Soviet leadership. Assuming that such develop-ments occurred in the next ten or so years, the USSR could enter the next century with much greater strength and spirit. If aided by events in various parts of the Third World and by ineffective or inadequate Western policies, the twenty-first century could witness substantial gains by the USSR in its global position and a much more severe challenge to U.S. security.

The greatest potential prize is Europe. A more powerful Soviet Union should be able to exercise far tighter control of the recalcitrant nations of Eastern Europe. Dealing from a

stronger hand in this scenario, Soviet leaders
could enforce greater discipline on the leaders
and people of East European nations and assure
greater conformity to Soviet political and
economic guidelines. If such persuasion were
insufficient, the Soviet Union would be in a much
better position to intervene directly with
military forces to ensure such conformity.

A Soviet position of strength in Eastern
Europe, particularly if it had been attained
without recourse to overt military intervention,
also might make possible the partial
accomplishment of long-standing Soviet goals in
Western Europe. In this alternative strategic
environment we postulate the demilitarization,
neutralization, and reunification of Germany.
Building on the renewed sense of common identity
so evident in Germany in recent years and on
continuing differences between German and U.S.
perceptions of the best policies to ensure
security in the nuclear age, powerful movements in
both parts of Germany could emerge that sought
withdrawal from NATO and the Warsaw Pact and
subsequent reunification. A failure in the German
economic recovery could contribute to such a
development, particularly if a faltering German
economy were juxtaposed against sustained
recoveries in the United States and East Asia
based on technological advances not available in
Central Europe.

The Soviet Union certainly would encourage
the emergence of such a movement in the Federal
Republic as a means of disrupting relations
between the United States and West Germany.
Should the movement gain control of a German
political party and eventually the West German
government, it is difficult to predict whether the
USSR would permit East Germany to withdraw from
the Warsaw Pact and unite with the Federal
Republic as a neutralized state (along the lines
of the Austrian model). Soviet leaders could see
economic benefits in such a move--expecially in
greater access to Western technologies and
capital--and a relative military gain; West
Germany's contribution to NATO is far greater than

is East Germany's contribution to the Warsaw Pact.
The neutralization of Germany would constitute a
very major step toward the destruction of NATO and
the withdrawal of U.S. power from Europe. This
has long been a primary objective of Soviet
foreign policy, as it would create conditions in
which the USSR could dominate Europe politically.

On the other hand, the USSR's leaders would
be concerned about the long-run implications of
such a development. It can be assumed that Soviet
leaders would never agree to the unification of
Germany unless the new state were effectively
demilitarized. Nevertheless, any such agreement
could not be enforced indefinitely and eventually
a united Germany could again turn into a powerful
military threat to the USSR. The successful
effort by Soviet leaders in 1984 to force
cancellation of the planned visit by the East
German leader Erich Honneker to Bonn demonstrates
their concern about any moves toward German
reunification. (Some West Europeans, notably the
French, also might oppose German unification.)

In most circumstances, the USSR would not
permit the creation of a unified Germany. In the
circumstances postulated for this strategic
environment, however, it is not inconceivable that
a renewed Soviet leadership, presiding over a
surging Soviet economy and a newly consolidated
Soviet position in Eastern Europe, might be
willing to take such a gamble. In effect, Soviet
leaders would be betting that the USSR's great
military strength would permit it to dominate the
newly unified German state politically, thus
preventing any move toward the remilitarization of
the new entity. They would be wagering further
that the economic, military, and political
benefits that would accrue to them from the
decoupling of the Federal Republic from NATO
(notably, the eventual withdrawal of U.S. forces
from the Continent) would outweigh any long-term
risk posed to Soviet security.

If West Germany did withdraw from NATO, the
United States would have to reconsider fundamental
elements of its security policy. As postulated in

this strategic environment, the remaining members of the alliance would seek to fall back to defensive positions that were focused on France. The United States would continue to commit itself to the defense of Western Europe and would maintain substantial forces in Europe to make credible that guarantee, with the largest portion based in France and Britain. Faced with Germany's defection, France would again integrate its armed forces into the alliance's military structure and permit the stationing of U.S. forces on its territory.

Beneficial events (from the Soviet perspective) also might occur on the USSR's southeastern border in this alternative strategic environment; in fact, the emergence of a less hostile, or at least less threatening, China would be a not unlikely development under certain circumstances. As noted previously, the course of events in China following Deng Xiaoping's rule is far from certain. Much would depend on how much time he had had to install individuals in key party and government positions that share his pragmatic policy preferences and understanding that far-ranging reforms are necessary if China is to conquer its severe economic disabilities. Many other factors would contribute to the future course of events in China, including the effects of weather on the harvests, the success of the campaign to curb population growth, and the continuing tolerance of the Chinese Army with regard to the rate at which it receives more modern military equipment.

It is certainly possible, and more likely sooner rather than later, that the Chinese economy would fail significantly, thereby resulting in serious political unrest. Domestic turmoil could result from many other causes as well, including a struggle for power among the army leadership, government technocrats, and party officials in the aftermath of Deng's death. The potential victor in such a struggle is hard to predict. A pro-Soviet faction seeking ideological orthodoxy and to recreate close ties between China and the USSR could emerge. Indeed, the economic and political successes postulated for the USSR in this scenario could only increase the prospects for the ascendance of a pro-Soviet faction. Once in power, such a Chinese government would quickly negotiate a border settlement that permitted the redeployment of large numbers of Soviet troops. Even if of such an eventuality never came to pass, a tumultuous China racked by internal political conflict, uncertain of its economic future, and unable to play a commanding role in Southeast Asia would constitute a.lesser threat to Soviet interests and permit the USSR to devote greater attention (and resources) to other parts of the world.

Finally in this difficult scenario, we assume several significant opportunities for the aggrandizement of Soviet interests in various parts of the Third World, especially the reversal of the Arab-Israeli conflict--probably following Egypt's decision to step away from its peace treaty with Israel and resume an active role as a confrontation state. Several events might precipitate such a decision, including a perception on the part of Egyptian leaders that they were losing control of the population to radical leaders, or actions by Israel toward the occupied territories that forced the Palestinian issue. Regardless of cause, a renewal of Arab-Israeli conflict could provide substantial opportunities for the extension of the Soviet military and political influence in the Middle East and the escalation of dangers to U.S. security and economic interests.

A second danger spot in this alternative strategic environment could be southern Africa, where the emergence of substantial violence both within South Africa and between South Africa and bordering nations would be a distinct possibility. Any such development could pose serious risks to Western sources of some strategic minerals.

The Caribbean and Central America offer a third region in which Soviet interests might be greatly enhanced in this alternative environment. In the absence of effective U.S. actions, major

advances by Marxist-Leninist regimes could be made
in the region. In addition to Nicaragua,
El Salvador, Guatemala, Honduras, Panama, Haiti,
and several additional Caribbean islands could
fall victim to Cuban-supported revolutionary
movements. If left-wing movements were successful
in many of these countries, political instability
also might spread to Mexico, with unpredictable
results. Moreover, if the United States did not
react decisively to these setbacks, Soviet leaders
might be tempted to develop gradually their own
military facilities in the region, something they
have avoided so far in the case of Nicaragua.

In sum, the composite future presented in
this alternative would be a very dangerous one for
the United States. It would provide a severe
test, looking twenty years into the future, of
U.S. general purpose and theater nuclear forces.
In effect, this scenario envisions a Soviet Union
poised to achieve its most important geopolitical
objective--dominance of the Eurasian landmass--and
capable of enhancing its position in regions of
the Third World that are vital to U.S. interests.
All would not yet be lost to the United States if
this strategic environment were to become a
reality, but it would be a long and uphill
struggle to regain a more secure position in world
affairs. Much would depend in this scenario upon
the performance of the U.S. economy and the
willingness of the U.S. population to devote
considerable resources to a sustained defense
buildup. Given the defection of West Germany,
preventing Soviet domination of the remainder of
Western Europe would represent a severe challenge
requiring substantial increases in the amount of
resources devoted to NATO's defense on the part of
all the remaining members, but realistically, also
requiring decisive U.S. leadership. Accelerated
development of the emerging technologies described
in Chapter 2 could contribute measurably to a
satisfactory outcome, but it seems very unlikely
that conventional forces alone would be sufficient
to restore a credible deterrent posture. U.S.
leadership also would be required to maintain the
alliance with Japan in this scenario and to
prevent the renewal of close Sino-Soviet ties; a

strengthened U.S. military position in Asia and the Pacific would be a prerequisite for effective action. Finally, dealing with Soviet inroads in the Middle East, southern Africa, and Central America could greatly stress U.S. naval and other maritime capabilities, placing additional demands on defense resources.

Implications for U.S. Military Planning

It is obvious that U.S. planners in this strategic environment would have to refocus on the Soviet Union and the greatly enhanced threats it posed to U.S. interests and objectives. Given an erosion of the U.S. position throughout the world, primary emphasis should be placed on ensuring the security of United States' territory by strengthening and modernizing strategic nuclear forces. Efforts to develop effective strategic defenses also should be accelerated significantly. If the technology appeared promising, there could be initial deployments of the beginnings of a major missile defense system before the end of the century. The consensus of our technological experts, however, is that sufficient development of the necessary technology would be unlikely during this time period. In view of the probable squeeze of the defense budget this might mean a deferral of any deployment decision. As dramatic changes would be taking place in both Europe and Asia, as well as in parts of the Third World, each of which would place demands for greater military capabilities, difficult decisions about priorities would have to be made even if substantially greater resources were allocated to the armed forces.

The neutralization of Germany would cause a basic rethinking of U.S. policies toward Europe. It is not at all inconceivable that the realignment of German policy would prompt the United States to embrace an isolationist policy or to shift toward a strategy focused heavily on the Pacific, thereby leaving the nations of Europe to fend for themselves. Such a basic shift in U.S. strategy also could include a decision to rely more heavily on nuclear forces, perhaps in association with the eventual strategic defense of this nation and its key remaining allies.

France's willingness to resume the stationing of U.S. forces on French soil, however, and a commitment for greater resource allocations to defense by several European governments might induce the United States to maintain the NATO alliance. The use of French territory would make possible a defense in depth for NATO, but the French could not replace West Germany's military contribution to the alliance, particularly in ground forces. NATO thus might be compelled to pay increasing attention to nuclear strategies and, in effect, compensate for its significant loss of conventional forces by raising the stakes of any new conflict in order to strengthen the deterrent value of the now smaller forces.

Assuming that the United States did attempt to maintain the NATO alliance, emphasis in U.S. military deployments would have to swing between Europe and Asia, depending on the situation at any one time. If Sino-Soviet ties improved and deepened during the years, the United States would be faced either with the freeing of substantial Soviet forces now deployed on the Chinese border for use elsewhere, particularly in Europe, or with a renewed Chinese threat to friendly nations and U.S. interests in Asia, or both. Presumably, the Japanese would allocate much larger amounts of resources to defense in this environment, thereby making possible a significant extension of Japanese military capabilities.

As a result of these developments, the United States would have to recruit and equip larger general purpose forces. Given the fluidity of the situation in Eurasia, most of these forces would have to be based in the United States and provided with the capability to deploy rapidly anywhere in the world. Airlift, fast sealift, and sea control forces all would have to be strengthened measurably. Naval forces deployed in the Caribbean would have to be expanded as well. Because direct Soviet military intervention in virtually any contingency would be a far greater risk in this environment, U.S. forces (and the equipment provided to U.S. allies) would have to be more sophisticated and capable of defeating a more advanced foe. The option of utilizing more lightly equipped forces for Third World contingencies would be more risky in this strategic environment than in the two described previously.

Terrorism would be a serious problem in this environment, as in the previous ones, but relative to the threats posed by the USSR the demands posed by terrorist contingencies would be minor. There would be a greater tendency within the United States toward unilateralism and isolationism, given the failure of our previous European policy. To compensate for this and to demonstrate that we were not cowed by Soviet expansionism, U.S. officials could well become more aggressive, thus placing greater demands on the military establishment. In the end, however, very difficult decisions concerning priorities almost certainly would have to be made. Unless the U.S. population (and allied nations) were willing to support the armed forces on an almost wartime footing, it is difficult to see how all U.S. commitments could be sustained in the face of such adverse developments in international political/military relationships.

ALTERNATIVE FOUR: AN ANARCHIC ENVIRONMENT

The fourth composite future incorporates radical changes in the structure of those international relationships that have dominated world politics since the end of World War II. It is probably also the most dangerous environment, even though it postulates a greatly reduced threat from the Soviet Union. To construct this environment, we have assumed that the Soviet people would eventually lose patience with the many failures of Soviet leaders and the continual thwarting of their own national and human aspirations, which would lead to a condition of chronic turmoil and some violence within the USSR itself. Simultaneously, however, we also have assumed the breakup of the U.S. system of alliances and the emergence of independent, nationally-minded, and nuclear-armed industrial powers in Europe and Japan. According to this scenario, current trends toward economic protectionism, the decline of international organizations, and nationalism continue and accelerate. The United States eventually returns to isolationist policies, renouncing most of its existing security commitments. With this complex and uncertain structure of relations and with the tumultuous situations also envisioned in the Third World, the possibility of major conflict eventually involving the United States would be extremely high.

Future events in Eastern Europe and the USSR would be particularly unpredictable. How long disorders such as those postulated in this scenario could continue in the Soviet Union without provoking some sort of desperate response on the part of the Soviet armed forces or political authorities is impossible to predict. During the period of unrest, the threat posed by the Soviet Union to other nations might be diminished greatly. None of the experts interviewed for this study credited the commonly expressed theory that a besieged Soviet leadership might lash out in a move to divert attention at home and bolster the leadership's position with a military triumph. But radical external actions by Soviet leaders faced with a rapidly deteriorating domestic situation have to be considered a possibility nonetheless.

Although relations between the United States and the new defense entity in Europe might not necessarily be adversarial, the French-led alliance would seek to demonstrate its independence of the United States and, pointedly, its neutral position in relation to the United States and USSR, which could lead to economic and political conflicts if not military difficulties. The European defense entity would depend on threats of immediate nuclear escalation as the primary element in its defense posture because it could not possibly compete with the USSR to maintain an adequate balance of conventional forces.

European forces on both sides of what again might be called the Iron Curtain would be maintained in a high state of readiness, given the inevitable tension. A massive Soviet action to crush Eastern Europe--and thereby eliminate the primary inspiration of its own domestic dissidents--is a significant possibility. Any such action, of course, could spill over easily into the West. A similarly unpredictable situation would prevail in East Asia. Japan can be expected to rearm and thus acquire nuclear weapons (not a completely farfetched possibility according to the proliferation experts) and to pursue a foreign policy independent of the United States. Such a development would shatter the relative stability that now characterizes relations in the region and result in tense Sino-Japanese and Soviet-Japanese relations. Were it not for the USSR's domestic troubles and those on its Western borders, a decisive Soviet action to nip the new Japanese threat in the bud--perhaps by imposing its own control on Korea, Manchuria, and portions of northern China--is certainly within the realm of possibility. Nations on the margins of these great power struggles would seek protection somewhere. Whether they would ask the United States for security guarantees or try to develop a security relationship with one of their closer neighbors would probably depend upon how far U.S. isolationism had proceeded already and what the early consequences of this shift in U.S. policy had been for other nations that depended on U.S. security guarantees.

The rest of the world would witness violence and bloodshed on a major scale and the pursuit by all nations of whatever nuclear options were available to them. The likelihood that one or more nuclear wars might actually take place before the end of the century would be high. The United States might continue to support a few of its closest allies in the Middle East or Africa, but nuclear threats would be very close to the surface of any commitment we made abroad. More extensive U.S. involvement could probably be expected in the Western Hemisphere, but even here policy may well have to include a nuclear component, given the proliferation forecast for Brazil and Argentina.

An environment such as that described in this anarchic scenario would be short-lived. The scope and intensity of likely conflicts would be so great and the political instabilities so sharp that the pattern of international relations described here seems almost certain to be transformed into something else within a few years, such as the creation of broader European and Asian coalitions, resulting in a sort of Orwellian tripartite international system. Or, assuming that a strong leader emerged in the USSR and that major nuclear war had been avoided in Eurasia, the Soviet Union could reassert itself and, in the absence of U.S. power, gain dominance of the entire Eurasian landmass, including the Middle East. This would leave the two hemispheres--one led by a renewed Soviet Union, the other by the United States--as the only significant powers in world affairs. Still other scenarios are poissible, and a world-wide nuclear conflagration is far from the least likely.

The ability of the United States to defend its interests in such an international environment would depend on many factors, such as how quickly we could develop certain military technology (and exactly how capable it might prove to be). Technology that promises effective defenses against nuclear-armed missiles would be the most important aspect of this uncertainty, but other military capabilities could be importantly expanded as well. At the same time, the willingness of the U.S. people to sacrifice for their own defense might he a mediating factor in the evolution of this environment. Although the withdrawal of U.S. forces from Europe, Japan, and other areas would greatly reduce the cost of defense, the advanced technology necessary for effective defenses would be extremely expensive to develop and deploy on a large scale. In addition, given the global disorder that is likely to prevail, a sharp decline in economic output would be likely. International trade would decrease. Such basic resources as petroleum could become

more scarce and therefore more expensive. Fiscal
and trade cooperation among the industrial powers
would deteriorate. Debtor nations in the Third
World and Eastern Europe would almost certainly
repudiate their debts thus leading to the collapse
of the international financial system. The result
could be a severe economic crisis in this country,
just as we were seeking to increase defense
expenditures in order to deal with new threats to
our security.

Implications for U.S. Military Planning

Political and military developments like
those envisioned in this composite future would
necessitate a major reorientation of U.S. military
strategy. Demands for general purpose forces
would be greatly reduced, particularly the major
ground and air forces now planned for
contingencies in Europe. In their place, the
United States. could shift to a two tiered
strategy. First, there could be a crash effort,
similar to the Manhattan Project, to develop and
deploy systems capable of defending the United
States from missile attack. In view of the
emergence of additional nuclear-armed industrialized nations, the uncertain stability of
relationships, the high risk of war among the
great powers in Europe and Asia, and the lack of
effective U.S. military leverage in Eurasia
itself, all of which are postulated in this
scenario, the United States would essentially
have no alternative to protect its security.
Maintaining an effective and stable nuclear
deterrent in a bipolar world is difficult enough.
Attempting to pursue a deterrent strategy in a
world populated by four, five, or even six major
nuclear powers would be a most uncertain (and
insecure) course of action. Thus, the United
States almost certainly would do whatever possible
to accelerate the development and deployment of a
major defensive system. Whether such a crash
program would be successful or not, of course, is
unknowable. Nevertheless, there would be great
pressures to deploy whatever type of system were
available.

Initially, a defensive system might be deployed even if its capabilities were limited to defending against attacks by smaller nuclear powers and warding off the sort of ragged and limited attack produced by accidental or unauthorized launches. The tremendous proliferation of nuclear capabilities and the breakdown of alliances (and internal order in nuclear states) expected in this scenario could well make the deployment of defensive systems with even limited capabilities a prudent step, even if it could be taken only at great cost. Moreover, such a limited system could serve as a building block in the construction of a more extensive system capable of defending against more substantial attacks. The United States also would pursue the expansion of offensive nuclear forces as well as a largely maritime strategy to reassert its dominance in the Western Hemisphere, protect its interests (narrowly defined), and backup whatever security commitments were retained overseas. Heavily armed and technologically sophisticated naval strike forces, lightly armed ground units capable of rapid and decisive entry into trouble spots anywhere on the globe, appropriate lift and sea control forces, and long-range, land-based strike aircraft all could contribute to such a strategy. To the extent that the use of these forces were considered in Europe or Asia, however, they probably would have to be backed with tactical nuclear capabilities--at least as a deterrent.

ALTERNATIVE FIVE: AN OPTIMISTIC ENVIRONMENT

Finally, we might consider the military implications of a very optimistic, but still plausible composite future. In this case we assume that the United States maintains an activist foreign policy, and continues to deploy substantial armed forces in Europe and Asia in support of security commitments to the members of NATO, Japan, and South Korea, among others. We assume, moreover, as in the surprise-free forecasts, that despite continuing political and economic differences among their members and despite continuing fiscal and societal constraints on military options, these alliances manage to muddle through and maintain military forces and a degree of cooperation with each other and the United States which, if not fully satisfactory in the eyes of defense officials, at least are sufficient to dissuade potential adversaries from armed conflict in most circumstances.

We assume the surprise-free forecast in the case of the Soviet Union as well--a continuation of the current stagnant economy, a paralyzed political system, and a disaffected society. A few experts suggested that an even more negative projection of developments in the USSR may be plausible--the aggravation of these problems to the point of sustained internal disorders. This would be an unstable configuration, however. On the one hand, it might lead to sharp reversals in Soviet economic and foreign policies along the lines of those adopted by the Chinese: radical measures to decentralize the economic system and to create incentives for more productive individual behavior as well as a moderation of foreign and domestic political policies to encourage Western trade with, technological transfers to, and even investment in, the USSR. Such actions might be taken cynically, with the long-term plan of reverting to more aggressive policies once the economy had turned around, or such actions might represent a genuine change of heart among a new generation of Soviet leaders. On the other hand, an acute crisis within the USSR might lead to the emergence of a strong traditional leader able to consolidate his authority rapidly and to reassert a more aggressive foreign policy. In view of this second possibility, in terms of long-term U.S. security interests, a USSR continually on the verge of failure may be preferable to a USSR in which the failures of the economic and political systems were so overt as to compel reforms.

We do assume the most negative projection of events in Eastern Europe--sustained economic and political disaffection leading eventually to

violence in one or more nations. The USSR--
despite its weakened domestic situation--would
intervene militarily to reassert control. Any
such actions implicitly risk getting out of
control and leading to an East-West conflict.
Additionally, disorders in Eastern Europe would
have two major implications for Western security
interests. First, a Soviet Union preoccupied with
maintaining its military control of Eastern Europe
and preventing the dissension prevalent among its
allies from spreading more intensely to its own
population is unlikely to pose overt or immediate
threats to Western Europe, the Persian Gulf, or
other regions of interest to the United States.
There would be concern, of course, that a decaying
Soviet empire might lash out at its neighbors, and
preparations would have to be taken to deter any
such desperate gamble. But the physical demands
on Soviet forces and logistics generated by the
East European contingencies, the consequent
preoccupation of Soviet decisionmakers and policymaking processes, and the inevitable concern of
Soviet officials that other nations might take
advantage of the situation in Europe for their own
benefit all preclude an escalation of the Soviet
threat to Western interests. Second, any new
Soviet intervention in Eastern Europe also might
result in greater support in Western Europe for
more assertive policies and greater resource
allocations for defense. In the past, Soviet
interventions have had the effect of making the
Soviet military threat more tangible and the
concerns often expressed by Western defense
officials more credible. Even the Soviet-inspired
coup by the Polish armed forces and the
institution of martial law in Poland in 1982 had
the effect of turning opinion in France and other
nations toward greater support of more tough-
minded policies toward the USSR.

In East and South Asia we assume the
surprise-free forecast with a small variation.
China remains stable internally, progresses
economically, and remains tacitly allied with the
West. The troubled nations on the rim of the
region continue to develop economically and,
moreover, to progress toward more stable political

systems. Japan's prosperity continues, as does the nation's alliance with the United States. In addition, however, Japan allocates significantly greater resources to defense, thus building up its conventional military power significantly while remaining in close association with the United States and other democratic nations. (The continuing close association with the United States presumably would preclude Japan's acquisition of nuclear capabilities.)

Although not suggested by the experts interviewed for this study, several knowledgeable commentators on previous drafts considered this last possibility at least as plausible as a rearmed and independent Japan. Such a situation certainly would be beneficial from a U.S. perspective. Quite apart from the military power thus added to the Western position in the Pacific, Japanese rearmament within such a context would ameliorate the otherwise negative effect of a more powerful Japan on China and nations in Southeast Asia.

The surprise-free forecasts are also assumed for the Middle East and Africa, both of which offer relatively benign environments for U.S. military planning. In Central America, we assume that a vigorous U.S. policy manages to "roll back" the previous trend toward the extension of Marxist-Leninist regimes in the region. Although not likely to extend to Cuba itself (and not the most likely case by any means), such a development is feasible according to our experts.

Implications for U.S. Military Planning

The optimistic composite future would offer relatively fewer and less demanding challenges to U.S. security and thus could result in reductions in U.S. military forces. The projected greater contributions of European members of NATO and Japan would permit some reductions in U.S. forces deployed in those regions and, eventually, cutbacks in general purpose force levels. Favorable political developments in the Middle

East, South and East Asia, and Central America would defuse situations that otherwise--in the extrapolated environment, for example--might make incremental demands on U.S. general purpose forces. It also might be possible to reduce nuclear modernization programs and force levels in this environment if the Soviet Union's much weakened position made it possible to reach arms control agreements on relatively favorable terms.

Obviously, any reductions in U.S. forces could neither be made rapidly nor proceed too far during the forecast period. This environment is not the millennium by any means; military power would remain the ultimate guarantor of the nation's security and a key instrument in support of foreign policies. Events in several regions would remain unpredictable; prudence would dictate the maintenance of a strong force posture to assure the continued close cooperation of alliance partners, the deterrence of any Soviet adventures, and the continued favorable disposition of such key nonaligned nations as China. Moreover, there would continue to be threats in this international environment from terrorist groups and smaller hostile nations, such as Cuba and Iran, which would require specialized forces. Still, in time, if the international system described in this environment proved stable and lasting, it might be possible to negotiate formal political settlements to legitimize the evolution of events, and a range of arms control treaties to build confidence among former antagonists and to assure mutual reductions in forces. If so, by the next century the world could well be a more peaceful and less dangerous place.

5

Conclusions

It is only prudent to be tentative and cautious in forecasts of international events, particularly forecasts with as broad and distant a sweep as those in this study. In all probability, none of the alternative strategic environments described in the preceding chapter--not even an approximation of one--represents accurately the full pattern of global political/military relations that will emerge in the next century.

Twenty years is a sufficient period of time for completely new societal movements to be created and incubated and to influence events in particular nations or regions. No matter how many experts are consulted in preparing a forecast, on how knowledgeable those experts may be, there is always the possibility that somewhere--in the villages of South Asia or in the slums of South America or in the cities of Europe--a new system of beliefs or a new charismatic leader espousing an old belief system in new guise may now, unknown to us, be gaining strength and influence. When such a movement matures, as did the Islamic fundamentalist movement in the late 1970s, it can alter substantially the expectations of all outside observers, creating previously unthought of possibilities and uncertainties.

It also must be recognized that the five alternative strategic environments presented in this study represent "pure" cases and, as such, are unlikely to be realized fully. In effect,

154

they constitute straight-line extrapolations of one or another of the more salient current trends during the full forecast period. In reality, events do not proceed in such a direct fashion. There is a self-limiting factor in world politics. Each action tends to create a counteraction. Each social force tends to create a counterforce. Cumulatively, the impact of new forces tends to be blunted and diverted. Consider, for example, the current status of the international trends that dominated world politics in the late 1970s:

1. The successes of Islamic fundament-alism led to the reemergence of individuals espousing secular prag-matism and greater moderation in several Arab nations, which resulted in the repression or cooption of more radical elements. What seemed five to ten years ago to be an irresistible tide has at least been blunted, if not yet defeated.

2. Oil power, which in the 1970s was the dominant force in the world economy and apparently a powerful political instrument, resulted in greater energy conservation, the accelerated develop-ment of alternative sources of energy, and a global economic recession that depressed the oil market and greatly weakened the influence of the oil producers.

3. The expansion of Soviet influence in the Third World, which was seemingly unstoppable in the 1970s, resulted in fact in greater internal resistance to communist subversion on the part of several nations as well as more assertive U.S. policies and defense programs and, as pointed out in several of the regional sections, now is apparently being reversed.

Each new development thus altered the trendline but also led to the creation of counterforces that in turn influenced events and patterns of relationships, thereby causing the future environment to diverge less substantially from the original trendline than, at one point, might have appeared likely. Although events did not move as much in the direction that the original social force seemed to suggest, such major developments as the Islamic fundamentalist revolution or the advent of oil power clearly do make a difference. The emergence of counterforces is not sufficient to drive the trendline back to its original bearing, events move in some new, usually compromised, direction. Forecasting the future, as compared to describing plausible alternative futures, thus requires that the analyst go beyond the identification and extrapolation of key trends. He or she must somehow integrate the consequences of many competing social forces and events and forecast the net effects not only of those factors but also of the counterfactors that inevitably will emerge in response.

On the basis of all available evidence, the surprise-free forecast appears to this writer to be the most likely of the five alternative strategic environments. Nevertheless, the surprise-free forecast seems somewhat too pat--that is, too similar to the present pattern of international politics. Somehow, intuitively, the surprise-free extrapolation seems to discount the ultimate impact of extant economic, demographic, and technological trends on political relation-ships. If the reader will indulge, I would like to express a personal view of the likely future pattern of international relationships at the end of the century.

The surprise-free forecast does seem about right for the Soviet Union. From all available evidence, the USSR's internal problems are so severe as to exert major constraints on that nation's ability to pursue an effective or aggressive foreign policy for the rest of this century and beyond. At the same time, given the pervasiveness of the Soviet internal security system and certain attitudes of the Soviet people, it seems unlikely that these problems will lead to serious internal unrest and disorders. There is, of course, the possibility that fundamental reforms of the Soviet political and economic systems could be implemented or that a desperate attempt by the Soviet leadership cadre to override domestic problems by creating international crises might be made. In the writer's view, however, there is little empirical reason to consider either alternative as more than a remote possibility.

The European forecast appears to be the most understated with regard to potential changes in fundamental relationships. There do seem to be very basic divergences in perspectives on foreign and defense policies emerging between U.S. and West Europeans populations--divergences that are accentuated when the attitudes of younger generations are examined separately from those of their elders. Moreover, the alliance seems to be moving into an ever narrowing space regarding its strategic options; tightening financial and political constraints on NATO's defense choices seem to be hardening, therby making it more and more difficult for the alliance to define a credible posture. The Warsaw Pact faces even more difficult problems, as the resilience of East European nationalism portends continuing problems for the Soviet Union in defining a satisfactory relationship with its erstwhile allies. The results of these trends are unlikely, in the author's view, to be as dramatic as the reunification of Germany or the total withdrawal of U.S. military power from the Continent--at least not in the relatively short period examined in this forecast. Nevertheless, a gradual loosening of military ties within the two alliances and a coincident dampening of the military competition between NATO and the Warsaw Pact seem a credible forecast.

One can almost imagine a "settlement" of the long postwar struggle for Europe. Such a settlement would include tacit recognition of the permanence of the formal demarcation of the Continent between opposing social systems but coincident recognition of the necessity of maintaining a stable, peaceful, and permeable East-West boundary. In such circumstances, there could develop a very rich and complicated system of interconnections between East and West in Europe and far greater independence for the nations of Eastern Europe--at least in the economic policies they choose to pursue and in their relative freedom to promote their own national cultures and styles of political expression. Such a settlement also implies a reduction of U.S. influence in the West and the region's effective withdrawal as a source of contention between the United States and the Soviet Union. It does not, however, imply the Continent's Finlandization, in the pejorative sense that term denotes. It means that within the formal system of alliances, Europeans will come to be the masters of their own fortunes, free to determine their own economic policies and internal political arrangements, with the influence of both the United States and the Soviet Union greatly reduced.

I am far less optimistic about the future course of events in East Asia. Here, two grave uncertainties--the future policies and orientation of China and Japan--depend mainly on internal developments in those nations but importantly also on the future effectiveness of U.S. policies. None of the experts, and certainly not this writer, feels sufficiently confident to predict the future course of affairs in China. It must suffice to note that a substantial change in that nation's currently pragmatic domestic policies and relatively moderate foreign policies would have the most severe implications, not only for the future course of events in the region but also for the most basic power relationships on a global scale. As for the future of Japanese policies, as in the case of Western Europe one must wonder whether changing attitudes on the part of younger generations must not eventually lead to reordered national priorities--in this case toward a greater emphasis on national military power. If so, then the issue of whether such capabilities are developed within a framework of close U.S.-

Japanese relations or in support of an independent Japanese foreign policy becomes crucial. In view of the trend toward greater economic and technological competition between the United States and Japan (and other nations in East Asia), greater Japanese independence is more likely than not, and if this guess is accurate, then there is a potential for considerable discord in the future.

In South Asia there are a number of uncertainties with substantial potential for violent change. The strength of Islamic fundamentalism in Iran and Pakistan, the ongoing struggle between Iran and Iraq, the continuing insurgency in Afghanistan, the centrifugal forces in India, and Pakistan's efforts to acquire nuclear weapon capabilities (and the consequent implication of an Indian-Pakistani nuclear arms competition within this century) all portend tremendous instabilities, radical political change, and, should these trends lead to direct Soviet intervention or threaten the oil-producing areas, the possibility of U.S. involvement in military conflict.

Elsewhere in the Middle East (including North Africa), I would agree that prospects are improving. There seems to be a trend toward pragmatism and moderation that can benefit the United States in important ways. The crucial variable here, however, is the future course of events in Egypt. As in the case of China and Japan, U.S. policies can make important contributions in assuring favorable outcomes.

The experts' forecasts also seem reasonable for other Third World regions. Most of the nations of South America seem to be on the road toward more stable political systems and renewed economic development; continued success in resolving the debt crisis and future events in Brazil are crucial. Sub-Saharan Africa, on the other hand, seems to be mired hopelessly in a deteriorating situation; economic and political prospects in much of that Continent seem particularly grim. The situation in the south, moreover, weighs heavily on the future course of

events in the region. Given the apparent
attitudes of the majority of the white population
in South Africa, it is difficult to foresee a
peaceful resolution of the situation. If this
forecast proves accurate, it can only portend even
more pessimistic economic and political prospects.

Such a strategic forecast has important
implications for U.S. military planning, not the
least of which is the possibility of a deemphasis
of strategic offensive forces (presumably through
the vehicle of negotiated mutual reductions in
U.S. and Soviet forces). This forecast also
suggests the possibility of substantial with-
drawals of U.S. troops from Europe and gradual
reductions in U.S. general purpose forces intended
for European contingencies. At the same time,
this scenario implies substantial incremental
needs for U.S. general purpose forces for South
and East Asian contingencies. One need not
foresee the actual involvement of the United
States in military conflicts in those Asian
regions to reach such a conclusion. If events
develop in as calamitous a fashion as seems
feasible in South Asia, substantial, applicable
U.S. military power will be necessary simply to
deter adversaries from taking advantage of the
situation and to exert a certain amount of
diplomatic leverage. If developments in China and
Japan should proceed adversely, a strong U.S.
military posture might be helpful in defining a
new relationship among the great powers in the
region that can help to protect vital U.S.
interests.

In general, we are likely to observe a
continuing diffusion of global power in the next
twenty years. Despite its great military power,
the Soviet Union will not dominate events, nor
despite its great military power and tremendous
economic leverage, will the United States. If
anything, there is likely to be a further leveling
of national power. Most projections predict that
the United States will produce about 20 percent of
the world's gross national products by the year
2000, a drop of 5 points from current figures.
Militarily, the continuing proliferation of

nuclear weapons capabilities and advanced conventional weapons technologies must, in time, tend to restrict the abilities of the great powers to dominate world events--or at least to do so with impunity.

A recent trend toward accelerated international entropy has been noted frequently by many analysts. Indeed, it seems, based on this study as well, that there are tendencies toward reduced international cooperation, a weakening of international institutions, economic protectionism, more independent foreign policies, and frequent recourse to military force. For better or worse, these trends seem likely to continue. They suggest that the world will continue to be a violent and dangerous place--one in which military power will play, as at present, vital and legitimate roles in the defense of the nation's interests.

Appendix A: Delphi Panels for Technological and Proliferation Forecasts

Modified Delphi techniques were used to develop the forecasts of both military technologies and nuclear proliferation in order to elicit a consolidated view from a group of experts without subjecting them to group dynamics that sometimes can prejudice the results of meetings. In the Delphi methodology, forecasts are developed strictly through correspondence. Panel members are asked an open-ended question at first. Their responses are tabulated, and the aggregate results are sent to each panelist. Respondents are then given an opportunity to alter their responses in view of the overall results or to explain their positions. The basic question can be narrowed at this juncture, as well, by specifying particular assumptions that should govern responses.

MILITARY TECHNOLOGY

We asked twenty-two distinguished scientists and technologists, all of whom have had experience within the Defense Department or have sat on defense advisory committees, "Which potential technological developments, in your opinion, would have a significant impact on U.S. national security?" The question was posed with deliberate vagueness so as to encourage wide-ranging responses that addressed developments in military technologies and developments in other areas that could influence military planning. The results of the first Delphi round were disappointing in the

164

case of the technological forecast. Only two-thirds of the initial panelists responded, thus leaving gaps in the scientific specialties covered. Given this poor response and the fact that the answers that were received were disparate in content and approach, a second round was foregone. Consequently, the results of the written responses were supplemented with several interviews and studies that had been prepared previously to generate the forecasts described in Chapter 2. A list of the individuals partici-pating in both aspects of the process follows:

> Anonymous, a very senior U.S. scientist interviewed for the study requested that he remain anonymous.
> Ardent Bement, Jr., TRW Inc.
> Paul Berenson, Defense Science Board
> James Burnett, TRW Inc.
> Seymour Deitchman, Institute for Defense Analyses
> John Deutsch, Massachusetts Institute of Technology
> Sidney Drell, Stanford University
> Alexander Flax, Institute for Defense Analyses
> Charles Herzfeld, ITT Corporation
> Joshua Lederberg, The Rockefeller University
> Michael May, Livermore National Laboratory
> William Perry, Hambrecht and Quist
> Samuel Tennant, The Aerospace Corporation
> Leonard Sullivan, Systems Planning Corporation
> Charles Zraket, The MITRE Corporation

NUCLEAR PROLIFERATION

A panel of fifteen individuals was estab-lished for the nuclear proliferation forecast. All are well known experts in the field; many have worked within the government on these problems. They were asked, "In addition to the five declared nuclear powers, by the year 2010, which nations are likely to have (1) acquired a substantial nuclear stockpile (at least one hundred weapons); (2) demonstrated a capability to detonate a

nuclear device; and (3) achieved, but not
declared, a nuclear capability. All but one of
the panelists responded in the first round, and
named a total of twenty-five nations in one of the
three categories. As the panelists were quick to
point out, however, proliferation forecasts depend
heavily on assumptions concerning the parameters
of the international environment during the period
in question. The panelists therefore were sent
the results of the first-round survey with
directions to name countries in the second round
that by the year 2000 were likely to fall in one
of two categories: had achieved a nuclear weapons
capability (with or without actually having
detonated a device); or had accumulated a
stockpile of at least one hundred weapons. In
addition, the panelists were told to assume that
there would not be any sort of nuclear war before
the end of the century and that the United States
would continue to play an active role in world
affairs. These two assumptions had been
identified by the panelists in the first round as
the most critical ones. Finally, a "nuclear
weapons capability" was defined more precisely
than it had been in the first round. Thirteen
panelists responded in the second round with the
results that are summarized in Chapter 2. The
members of the proliferation panel are listed
below:

Richard Betts, Brookings Institution
Albert Carnesale, Harvard University
Warren Donnelly, Congressional Research
    Service
Rodney Jones, Center for Strategic and
    International Studies
Myron Kratzner, International Energy
    Associates
Steven Meyer, Massachusetts Institute of
    Technology
Joseph Nye, Harvard University
William Potter, University of California at
    Los Angeles
George Quester, University of Maryland
George Rathjens, Massachusetts Institute of
    Technology
Robert Seldon, Los Alamos National Laboratory

166

Gerard Smith, Consultants International Group
Leonard Spector, Carnegie Endowment for
   International Peace
Charles Van Doren, Consultant
Kenneth Waltz, University of California at
   Berkeley

Appendix B: Experts Interviewed for Regional Forecasts

Nearly sixty individuals were interviewed in the course of preparing the regional forecasts presented in Chapter 3. Three asked to remain anonymous; all were promised that specific remarks would not be attributed to them.

GLOBAL PERSPECTIVES

Richard Barnet, who is a commentator and writer on contemporary international issues, has long been affiliated with the Institute for Policy Studies in Washington.

Zbigniew Brzezinski was assistant to President Jimmy Carter for national security affairs; Mr. Brzezinski is now affiliated with the Georgetown Center for Strategic and International Studies.

William Cline is a senior fellow at the Institute for International Economics, and has written extensively on the international debt crisis and other economic issues.

Alexander George worked at the RAND Corporation before joining the faculty of Stanford University.

Andrew Goodpaster has had a distinguished career in the U.S. Army, including service as military assistant to President Dwight Eisenhower, director of the Joint Staff, and NATO supreme allied commander in Europe.

Joseph Kraft was a nationally syndicated columnist for twenty-five years.

Edward Luttwak, an analyst and commentator on international security issues, is now affiliated with the Georgetown Center for Strategic and International Studies.

Robert McNamara was secretary of defense during the Kennedy and Johnson administrations; he also served as president of the World Bank for ten years before he retired.

Harold Malmgren, an economist specializing in trade and technology issues, runs a consulting firm in Washington.

Admiral Thomas Moorer served as both chief of naval operations and as chairman of the Joint Chiefs of Staff during the 1970s; he is now retired.

Robert O'Neill, an Australian national, is director of the International Institute for Strategic Studies in London.

Nelson Polsby is a member of the faculty of the University of California at Berkeley; he is an authority on the U.S. political system.

James Schlesinger has served, among other government posts, as the director of central intelligence, secretary of defense, and secretary of energy. He is now affiliated with the Georgetown Center for Strategic and International Studies.

William Schneider who is associated with the American Enterprise Institute, is an expert on U.S. public opinion.

W. Y. Smith retired from the U.S. Air Force in 1983 after a career that included service as assistant to the chairman of the Joint Chiefs of

Staff and deputy commander in chief of the European Command. He is now president of the Institute for Defense Analyses.

Cyrus Vance, now in private law practice, served as secretary of state under President Jimmy Carter and as deputy secretary of defense and secretary of the army during the Johnson administration.

EUROPEAN FORECAST

John Barry, a British citizen, works for Newsweek.

Christoph Bertram, formerly director of the International Institute for Strategic Studies, is now political editor of a German newspaper, Die Zeit.

Ian Davidson writes for London's Financial Times.

Richard Davies is an editor of the London Times.

Anders Ferm is the Swedish ambassador to the United Nations.

Pierre Hassner, a scholar of European political affairs, teaches at the University of Paris.

Stanley Hoffman writes primarily about European political affairs and is a member of the faculty of Harvard University.

Joseph Joffe, formerly a German newspaper editor, was affiliated with the Carnegie Endowment for International Peace at the time of the interview.

Catherine Kelleher teaches at the University of Maryland and writes on European political affairs.

Gert Krell, a German national, was affiliated with the International Institute for Strategic Studies at the time of the interview.

Robert Nurick, previously deputy director of the International Institute for Strategic Studies, is now at the RAND Corporation.

David Owen is currently the parliamentary leader of the British Social Democratic Party; he served as foreign minister during the last Labour government.

John Roper, formerly a member of Parliament, now edits the journal International Affairs for the Royal Institute for International Affairs. Theo Somer is the senior editor of Die Zeit.

Helmut Sonnenfeldt, now a scholar at the Brookings Institution, has held several senior posts on the staff of the National Security Council and at the State Department.

Specialist, a high-ranking member of the French government specializing in European political affairs.

Karsten Voight is a member of the Bundestag and a defense specialist with the German Social Democratic party.

William Wallace is deputy director of the Royal Institute for International Affairs in London.

SOVIET UNION FORECAST

Jeremy Azrael, now at the Department of State, taught and wrote about Soviet studies for many years at the University of Chicago.

Coit Blacker teaches at Stanford University.

Arnold Horelick has worked for many years at the RAND Corporation and served in the U.S. government during the Carter Administration.

William Hyland, now editor of the journal
Foreign Affairs (published by the Council on
Foreign Relations), retired in 1979 from a long
career in the U.S. government as deputy national
security adviser.

Specialist, an expert on the Soviet Union
working in the U.S. government.

Strobe Talbott is the Washington bureau chief
of Time Magazine.

Colonel Edward Warner retired from the U.S.
Air Force in 1982 and now works at the RAND
Corporation.

EAST AND SOUTH ASIAN FORECAST

Harry Harding, formerly on the faculty of
Stanford University, now works at the Brookings
Institution; he is primarily a China specialist.

Richard Holbrooke, now an investment banker
with Lehman Brothers, served as assistant
secretary of state for East Asian affairs during
the Carter administration.

Thomas Robinson, formerly with the RAND
Corporation, now teaches at Georgetown University;
he is an expert on Sino-Soviet relations.

Richard Solomon served on the staff of the
National Security Council during the Nixon and
Ford administrations and is now director of policy
planning at the State Department.

Specialist, an Asian specialist now working
in the U.S. government.

MIDDLE EASTERN FORECAST

Adhid Dawisha, an Iraqi national, was
teaching at the time of the interview at the

School for Advanced International Studies of the Johns Hopkins University.

Judith Kipper, formerly a journalist, is affiliated with the American Enterprise Institute.

William Quandt served on the staff of the National Security Council during the Carter administration; he is now affiliated with the Brookings Institution.

Harold Saunders, among other government posts, served as assistant secretary of state for Middle Eastern affairs during the Ford and Carter administrations; is now affiliated with the American Enterprise Institute.

AFRICAN FORECAST

Helen Kitchen writes on African affairs at the Georgetown Center for Strategic and International Studies.

Donald McHenry last served in the government as U.S. ambassador to the United Nations; he is currently affiliated with the Georgetown School of Foreign Service.

Alex Rondos, a British national, is the director of Catholic Relief Seervices in Cairo.

LATIN AMERICAN FORECAST

Mark Falcoff writes about Latin American affairs at the American Enterprise Institute.

Ed Gonzales, a Latin American specialist, teaches at the University of California at Los Angeles and also works at the RAND Corporation.

Robert Leiken writes about Latin American affairs at the Carnegie Endowment for International Peace.

Robert Pastor, a staff member of the National Security Council during the Carter administration, now teaches at the University of Maryland

David Ronfeldt, a Latin American specialist, is on the staff of the RAND Corporation.

Viron Vaky, last served during his distinquished career with the State Department as assistant secretary for Latin American affairs.